# Still Barred from Prison

# Still Barred from Prison

## Social Injustice in Canada

**Claire Culhane**

BLACK ROSE BOOKS   Montréal

Copyright 1985 ©
Black Rose Books Ltd.

**Third printing 1988**

Black Rose Books No. N88
ISBN Hardcover 0-920057-32-2
ISBN Paperback 0-920057-33-0

---

**Canadian Cataloguing in Publication Data**

Culhane, Claire, 1918-
    Still barred from prison

Includes index.
Bibliography: p.
ISBN 0-920057-32-2 (bound). ISBN 0-920057-33-0
(pbk.).

1. Prisons—Canada. 2. Criminal justice. Administration
of—Canada. 3. Prison violence—Canada.
I. Title.

HV9507.C86 1985          365'.971          C85-090076-X

---

Acknowledgement is made to the following for permission to
reprint excerpts from previously published material:

    Pulp Press — *Barred from Prison: A Personal Account*, 1979
    Black Rose Books — *1984 And After*, 1984

Editorial assistant: Linda Field

Cover design: John Sims

**Black Rose Books**
3981 boul. St-Laurent
Montréal, Québec H2W 1Y5

Printed and bound in Québec, Canada

This is to certify that Claire Culhane, a member of the Citizens' Advisory Committee of the B.C. Penitentiary, has been sitting with us, the Inmate Committee, since approximately 2 a.m. this morning and has observed every peaceful attempt we have made to have the simple opportunity to expose the insidious corruption in this institution; and the criminal intentional manner we are used over and over again by ambitious and evil men to further their greedy aims and political aspirations.

At the moment, this letter is being written because of the political corruption in this region and we honestly feel this mess may end worse than Attica.

We trust Claire Culhane, and if it should end as Attica ended, or worse, we feel certain she will take the facts to the public.

The only problem we see is, will the public listen even to her?

Inmate Committee
(B.C. Penitentiary)
September 26, 1976

# Contents

*There is no principle from which it follows that a pure unflawed democratic society must be permitted to continue tranquil and undisturbed, while it carries out criminal actions.*

Noam Chomsky

# Abbreviations

| | |
|---|---|
| C.A.C. | Citizens' Advisory Committee |
| C.A.P.C. | Canadian Association for the Prevention of Crime |
| C.D.C | Centre de Développement Correctionnel |
| C.I. | Correctional Investigator |
| C.J.S. | Criminal Justice System |
| C.P.B. | Community Prison Board |
| C.P.S. | Canadian Penitentiary Service |
| C.S.C. | Correctional Service of Canada |
| C.S.I.S. | Canadian Security Intelligence Service |
| E.P.O. | Emergency Power Order |
| F.L.Q. | Front de Libération du Québec |
| I.C. | Inmate Committee |
| I.E.R.T. | Institutional Emergency Response Team |
| I.P.S.O. | Institutional Preventive Security Officer |
| L.M.R.C.C. | Lower Mainland Regional Correctional Centre (Oakalla) |
| M.S. | Mandatory Supervision (parole) |
| N.P.B. | National Parole Board |
| O.D.D. | Office des Droits des Détenu-e-s (Québec-based) |
| O.W.C.C. | Oakalla Women's Correctional Centre |
| P.A.G. | Prisoners' Action Group |
| P.C.U. | Protective Custody Unit |
| P 4 W | Prison for Women (Kingston) |

| P.L. | Prisoner Liaison |
| P.R.C. | Prisoners' Rights Committee (Québec-based) |
| P.R.E.A.P. | Prison Research Education Action Project |
| P.R.G. | Prisoners' Rights Group (B.C.-based) |
| P.R.O.P. | Preservation of the Rights of Prisoners |
| P.S.A.C. | Public Service Alliance of Canada |
| P.S.R. | Penitentiary Service Regulations |
| Q.C.J.J. | Quaker Committee on Jails and Justice |
| R.C.M.P. | Royal Canadian Mounted Police |
| S.H.U. | Special Handling Unit |
| S.M.S.U. | Super Maximum Security Unit* |
| S.M.U. | Super Maximum Unit |
| V & C | Visiting & Correspondence (Dept.) |

---

* 'improved' name for the same unit (S.M.U.) following a 1975 B.C. Court declaration that the B.C. Penitentiary's solitary confinement unit was 'cruel and unusual punishment.'

# Chapter 1

# Why Another Book on Prisons?

*A right is not what someone gives you;
it's what no one can take from you.*

Ramsey Clark

# 1     Why Another Book
## on Prisons?

*The first step towards changing an environment is recognising its
potential or harm.*

Assault on the Worker: Occupational
Health and Safety in Canada, *1981*

This question is posed at a sombre and horrifying moment
in history, when the spectacle of millions dying in the wastelands
of Ethiopia is laid bare, as Orwell's 1984 draws to a close.

Climatologists warn that thirty million more Africans will
surely perish unless the land is immediately vacated. They
explain how human destruction of moisture-controlling plants
has been permitted to run rampant and must be halted (Toronto
*Globe & Mail*, November 7, 1984). For the next ten to fifty
years, refugee camps similar to those now filled with millions
of Palestinians must be established — yet another example of
a people driven from their homes. International government
and non-government organisations have been forewarned for
many years of this impending disaster.

Meanwhile, instant television, while galvanising some viewers
into action, tends to leave others cynical in a world where
many die from over-eating.

Canada's foreign aid programmes, not unlike those of the
United States, designate eighty per cent of their aid to im-
poverished countries as 'tied aid'. This means that it is not
an outright donation, but carries with it certain obligations,
such as the stipulation that the recipient purchase services and
supplies from the donor country. Policy-makers view aid programmes as a means of subtle intervention. By threatening to
withhold food aid, the 'donor' can manipulate the recipient
into accommodating the donor's economic and military interests.

"Since 1950, 130 countries have received food aid, with a
few strategic countries being the dominant recipients. Between
1968 and 1973, for example, South Vietnam received twenty
times more aid than the five African countries most seriously

affected by the Sahelian drought... foreign aid reinforces the power relationships that already exist" (*Aid as Obstacle*, 1980). "Food is... now one of the principal weapons in our negotiating kit," we are further assured by Earl Butz, U.S. Secretary of State for Agriculture, in *New State of the World Atlas, 1984.*

Keeping pace with the African disaster, according to the U.S. Arms Control and Disarmament Agency world military spending next year will top a trillion dollars (*The Gazette*, Montréal, May 17, 1984). To try and absorb the magnitude of this amount, consider that a trillion seconds works out to roughly 30,000 years.

At the same time that close to three billion dollars are being spent every day on the arms race — an estimated two million dollars *per minute* by the year 2000 (*The Facts*, May 1984) (with the U.S. leading and Canada reaping its rewards from the top ten spot in the line-up), one out of six North Americans — a total of thirty-eight million — is living below the poverty line. In these two affluent nations, young, unemployed, non-white, single men and women are the most affected. This same group also comprises the majority of the prison population.

We have come full circle... from the world information network portraying the dying in Africa, to the trillion dollars keeping the war coffers filled in order to boost the numbers of those yet to die, to the millions struggling to survive in the richest continent in the world.... The pandemonium extends across all borders and continues to eject human fodder in every direction, including directly into prisons — another aspect of the global failure of this century.

According to *The Times* (March 1979) "The state of prisons is becoming more and more depressing and no end to the misery seems in sight. The apparently inexorable decline of the prison system into near chaos is matched by the inability of the authorities involved to provide any relief." Also in 1979, Ramsey Clark, the only Attorney-General of the United States to oppose the death penalty, wire-tapping and prison construction and a self-confessed abolitionist, was a major speaker at The Incarcerated Offender Conference in Harrison Hot Springs, B.C. "Our prisons are a human disposal system," he informed the audience, saying that he would "...like to abolish the prison system as we know it... to achieve freedom, equality, and justice...." Clark also drew attention to the fact that "laws are political in nature" and that "those in power make the laws that contribute to social and economic inequalities" (*Matsqui News*, April 4, 1979). Since 1979, the record reflects only changes for the worse.

Why another book on prisons? To position the role of prisons in a violent society which responds with even more violence. To make it clear that until we accept the reality that prisons are the way we deal with our poor, our minority groups, and our unemployed, we tolerate them at our peril. Not until we absorb this truism and join others involved in combatting society's problems will there be any hope of salvaging our prison population, with its disproportionate number of Native Indians and a smaller but equally disadvantaged number of women.

Having determined that any rational explanation of the bedevilled prison system must ultimately be political, the short-term objectives of helping to keep prisoners alive are reviewed in this book.

Of paramount importance to prisoners is the preservation of maximum contact with their families, friends and lawyers in order to avoid the tragedy of becoming a 'missing' element. Any increase in the existing alienation makes prisoners even more susceptible to the physical and psychological abuse which has become the hallmark of prison life. Numerous studies emphasise the value of outside relationships and stress their positive contribution to solving the myriad of problems which may have led to the prisoner's initial conviction.

The Penitentiary Service Regulations (P.S.R.) repeatedly affirm this fact: "Visiting and Correspondence (V & C) privileges... shall be... in all circumstances calculated to assist in the rehabilitation and reformation of the inmate." But then it is left entirely to the discretion of the individual Warden to approve or disapprove of anyone who applies to visit and/or correspond. This 'privilege' (which is not a right) can be withdrawn without having to account to any person or body, not even to the three highest positions in the bureaucracy's pecking order — the Solicitor-General, the Minister of Justice, and the Commissioner of Corrections.

It is, then, not unusual that a potential visitor will be notified that according to Regulation 2.7, leave to visit and correspond has not been approved, since "...it is not considered necessary or desirable for the reformation and rehabilitation of the inmate... or the security of the institution." These reasons are not too different from those offered for 'awarding' Administrative Dissociation — segregation which consigns prisoners to 'the hole' — for indefinite periods. It is under this pretext alone, and not for any misdemeanour such as carrying contraband, that many 'active activists' are barred from visiting.

My story began with my participation in the B.C. Penitentiary Citizens' Advisory Committee (C.A.C.) during the 1976 hostage-taking, when it was learned that those in the Super Maximum area ('the hole') were being hosed down and deprived of food, clothing and heat by the guards, who were venting their anger on the only accessible victims — the remainder of the prison was controlled by the Inmate Committee. It was incumbent upon the C.A.C. to enforce the *Letter of Understanding* clause, namely, "to inform the public generally of conditions and issues arising within the institution." Not even after personally witnessing the wretched conditions could the Committee be persuaded to issue a press release. Following an unsubstantiated charge by the Administration that I had attempted to take prisoners' letters out, and the accompanying media furore, I was persuaded to resign from the C.A.C. The alternative presented the possibility that the entire C.A.C. might be asked to leave the prison at a time when its presence was crucial to the safety of the prisoners.

Two subsequent occupations of Wardens' offices to protest fresh violations of prisoners' rights resulted in convictions for criminal charges of illegal trespass of penitentiary land, and fines. My refusal to pay the fines resulted in their being written off. Shortly afterwards I was barred from further entry. Judicial measures to reinstate my visiting rights have yet to be tested in the Supreme Court of Canada. The ruling to bar me is enforced only in the Pacific Region (with a few exceptions). Even in the highest security levels, I am permitted to visit with prisoners everywhere else in Canada.

Far more ominous than members of the public being barred from entry into prisons is the pattern which emerges regarding the gradual but intimidating rendering of prisoners 'incommunicado.' The trend to curtail contacts leads to complete isolation during periods of crisis, including the denial of meetings with lawyers. It is in this context that citizens of Canada, analogous to other known repressive régimes, sometimes go 'missing', particularly when prisoners are transferred before being able to notify their relatives. Security precludes answering distressed calls, and it is not until the transferred prisoners receive their personal effects (address book, stamps, stationery) that they can make the necessary contacts to advise where they have been moved.

The warning has been sounded consistently by every investigative body following various explosive situations that denial of legitimate contacts during such incidents can assume macabre dimensions.

Attention is drawn to *Visiting and Correspondence* regulations over the past eight years:

**1976:** After being cleared by Security, one could visit as many prisoners as had placed one on their list.

**1978:** One could visit only one prisoner *per prison*, at the discretion of the Warden, except for families, who may have more than one member in the same prison.

**1980:** Visitors were reduced to the possibility of visiting only one prisoner *per region* — Atlantic, Québec, Ontario, Prairie, or Pacific.

**1982:** Visiting and Correspondence Applications included: "Are you now on another inmate's visiting list? If yes, state inmate's name, your relationship to him, and *which institution he is in*." (Emphasis added)

**1984:** The Visitors Information Package issued by the new S.H.U.* at Prince Albert quotes: "Visiting privileges will not be granted to an individual who... *is on the approved visiting list of another inmate in any correctional facility*... unless a direct

---

* Special Handling Unit — A minimum two-year programme of regulated solitary confinement in top security, heavily guarded, specially constructed prisons. 'Minimum' since any infraction adds to the time 'awarded' for solitary confinement. This process is not legally sanctioned by the courts, therefore it cannot be appealed.

family relationship exists between all three." (Emphasis added)

The implication is clear: visits to be permitted with only *one* prisoner in the entire length and breadth of this country. This ruling has been introduced in the most vulnerable area of prison life — the Special Handling Unit.

Before the reader embarks on a journey through the past decade of prison happenings in Canada, the power of language as it applies to the concentration of control must be clarified. The use of 'system' language which denies prisoners the reality of their own existence also serves to cloud public perception of life behind prison walls. In a military context, this is called 'winning the hearts and minds' of potential allies.

There may be no fancy turn of phrase to distinguish this book, but neither will there be any dishonest terminology, as in the following samplings:

The *Canadian Penitentiary System* (C.P.S.) is now officially called the *Correctional Service of Canada* (C.S.C.). However, people are still incarcerated in penitentiaries which still fail dismally to correct even the most outrageous features of the System or Service.

Convicted offenders are called *Inmates*, labelling them as institutionalised and powerless, instead of calling them *Prisoners* — persons temporarily deprived of their freedom and liberty, held captive.

*Feeding* is a participle which refers to the act of consuming nutrition. However, C.S.C. practice is to feature *feeding time* for prisoners, and *meal time* for everyone else.

The keepers in prisons and jails are *Guards* paid to guard prisoners and prevent them from escaping. They may be called *Correctional Officers, Classification Officers, Living Unit Officers, Case Management Teams, Parole Officers*, etc., but that does not change their role.

*Prisons* are places of confinement. Calling them *Correctional Centres, Facilities, Institutions, Reformatories, Pre-Trial* or *Remand Centres*, only camouflages their restrictive and secretive role.

*Health Care Officers* cover the wide spectrum of Doctors, Nurses, Social Workers, Psychologists, Psychiatrists — most of whom, save a few honourable exceptions, lack sufficient commitment or compassion to speak out effectively from their positions of power to expose the gross abuses.

The words *crime* and *criminal* are invariably related to street crime, but rarely, if at all, to other areas of criminality in our society. Setting aside the undisputed destruction of our environment on land, sea and air, as well as the insanities of the military-industrial complex, there is another type of crime which bears examining. "Every six hours a Canadian worker dies on the job and work-related injuries occur every seven seconds," in the period from 1973 to 1976, according to Reasons, *et al.*, in *Assault on the Worker* (1981). Profit-greedy industrialists who make the decisions to use unsafe and inappropriate but less costly equipment which places workers in danger are criminally negligent. However, under Canadian laws they are not liable for charges of first or second degree murder.

A swing away from the current call for the return of the death penalty would likely occur if the laws were changed to include murder charges against those responsible for the deaths of workers, and those who exploit the environment for profit while ignoring the ensuing deaths by poisoning or starvation.

*Solitary confinement* means being deposited in a cell approximately six by eleven feet for twenty-three hours a day. In the new S.H.U.'s, these may be more modern in construction, but they are still described by prisoners who endure them for weeks, months, and in some cases, years, as "being buried alive in an all-steel pressure-cooker." Antiquated vintage settings like St. Vincent de Paul, Dorchester, and the dungeons under the old cow barn at Oakalla, are all marked by the absence of furniture, bedding, plumbing and lighting, with a hole in the floor for a toilet. Segregation in the modern 1969 Archambault prison features the same toilet facilities, where the guards have their own way of controlling the flushing mechanism — backing up the faecal contents to flow all over the floor.

At Dorchester, the 'Chinese cells,' as they are also called, were considered in 1980 to be so totally unacceptable that the *Toronto Sun* (November 2, 1982) quoted the Correctional Investigator as saying, "They were absolutely filthy and human excrement was smeared on the walls, a definite health hazard. Unlit, unventilated, with only a hole in the floor for toilet purposes." That he was not exaggerating is supported by the

Solicitor-General, who confirmed that "...some of the Dorchester cells belong in another century."

The *hole* is referred to as *Administrative Dissociation, Segregation, Super Maximum,* and *Quiet Room* (for juvenile detention), but whatever it is called, it remains a prison cell characterised by 'insanity, fear and violence.' Its effects upon the prisoner are described by Dr. Richard Korn, a noted California criminologist, when testifying in a Canadian court in 1975:

> ...when he is capriciously removed from the only society he has... for reasons he knows not, for a duration he knows not... he passes into a nightmare. He becomes a non-person.... This process is foolproof... if you keep it up long enough it will break anybody.... *It is a form of murder....*
> (*Minutes of Proceedings*, No. 29, February 15, 1977)

Solitary confinement is written about in many languages, and will continue to be written about as long as human beings are imprisoned. From the pen of a young prisoner as a dear friend is committing suicide in the next cell:

> There is no natural light
> In the void
>
> black runs on and on
> and back into itself
>                          it is
> a black hole, absorbing
> like a sponge
>            and a drop of water
>
> wiped up and dissipated
> throughout the strands
> until there's nothing left
>
> of the drop
> once held a sparkle.
>
> (from *A Valediction to Shaun*, by Tom Elton,
>              Kent Institution, February 1982)

I offer no apologies for expanding upon the definition of solitary confinement, since there are no words in any language sufficiently eloquent to impress its meaning on those who still tolerate the perpetuation of this horror. The Canadian pattern of torture of prisoners in solitary confinement can easily qualify for the never-ending catalogue of human rights violations that are prevalent in countries such as Chile and Argentina during military rule.

The difficulty in finding some clue to the lawless prison system is not unlike the complexity which faces us as we search for answers to the many contradictions in the international body politic. The situation is exacerbated by the fact that prisoners do not possess the power to organise any significant resistance, mainly due to the severe restrictions and corruption in their environment. What is required, then, is that grassroots organisations work to expose, educate, and build resistance to the erosion of civil and human rights in the prison system. The straightforward use of language is a good beginning.

We must consider, too, how it is always the prisoners who clamour for open, public investigations, while it is always the prison Administrations which vigorously reject such inquiries. Would it be reasonable to suggest that prisoners with nothing to conceal have everything to gain from such a procedure, while the prison system has the most to lose under the gaze of public scrutiny?

It therefore becomes all the more incumbent upon those of us in the outside world to ensure that the rule of law is respected *inside* prisons. We should not lose sight of the fact that those same prisons have also been historically used to incarcerate people for reasons dictated by political events. Imprisonment has been likened to slavery, for like slavery it is imposed by one class on another.

Since the polemics of this book invite bias, let there be no doubt as to my position. It is a bias in favour of those who fight against the glaring injustices of the Canadian prison system, and, by extension, against injustice the world over.

# Chapter 2

# Prison Violence in Canada: A Predictable Pattern

*Most prisoners I know would rather be thought bad than mad. They say society may have a right to punish them, but not a hunting licence to remould them in its own sick image.*

Dr. Harvey Powelson

# 2    Prison Violence in Canada: A Predictable Pattern

*Societal problems cannot be solved by locking up people, or by pretending that those problems do not exist. Ultimately we are interested in a world without prisons; a world where transgressors are seen as a problem for everyone, not pariahs to be handed over to an archaic institution for removal from sight.*

Women Behind Bars, *1963*

## Oakalla

Not the naked reality of the B.C. Pen which I saw first-hand, not my research and readings on the subject, not my subsequent tours of prisons and personal contact with many prisoners, not any of these experiences shake me up like this sordid, grubby, miserable, hopeless mess called Oakalla. *(Barred From Prison*, 1979)

Five years later, there is no reason to depart from the above description. Personal contact with prisoners and their families and friends, through correspondence, phone calls and direct meetings, has maintained the flow of information, which has not noticeably changed.

Lower Mainland Regional Correctional Centre (Oakalla) is the largest of five provincial facilities in B.C. for those serving a 'deuce less one' (two years less a day). Located in Burnaby, this former farm lies adjacent to a lake and faces the mountains to the north. Oakalla includes a Maximum Security wing accommodating approximately 600 prisoners, and a separate compound, renamed Lakeside Correctional Centre for Women, housing approximately eighty. A panabode hut, suitable as a pre-release unit, and two other buildings are not in use, despite overcrowding and public criticism.

Oakalla continues to be the setting for fasts, suicides and riots, when media and concerned citizens are studiously barred from entering, and where citizens' committees must be appointed and approved by the Administration.

In July 1975, for the second time that year, 130 male prisoners staged a sit-down on the sports field to protest their abhorrent conditions and to draw attention to their demands. In spite of the realisation that 'in jail we have no rights,' their list included demands for freedom of speech and the right to be treated as human beings; a proper educational programme; job training; privacy in a dignified and relaxed visiting area; abolition of isolation; representation at internal disciplinary hearings with witnesses of their own choice; and the right to take part in the decision-making process.

In support of the non-violent sit-in, a small group of prison activists had gathered on the roof of a neighbouring private garage. The group's intention was to bear witness to any possible violence, and to reinforce the support coming in waves of chants from the women's gym: "We're with you! Stand firm!" The women prisoners, rarely allowed outdoors except for brief periods in their tiny 'play pen', had added the following demands: a complete investigation of medical facilities and staff incompetence made by an unbiased medical expert; better staff training and screening processes; better recreational facilities; and more adequate consideration of transfer choices.

After twenty-one hours, the men won three concessions before being herded back to their cells: a media tour; meetings between their Inmate Committee and the Administration accompanied by outside supporters; and the perennial 'no reprisals'. During the media tour, in the south wing once described as a 'throwback to colonial days when Oakalla held people in sheriff's custody,' no direct contact with prisoners was permitted. Despite this, those prisoners quite willing to be quoted by name poured out their grievances, fully aware that the listening guards would retaliate.

The tour was led through different areas of the prison, including a small classroom with several desks crowded closely together, where prisoners expressed their desire for more courses to accommodate the many who wanted to upgrade their schooling. The visitors also saw the Hospital Unit, which, they were told, provided free dental care, eyeglasses, prostheses and rhinoplasty. However, time did not permit any examination of charts to support this information. A former 'padded cell' was shown, which our guide claimed was no longer needed. "We now use chemical controls," he boasted, inadvertently divulging that new 'scientific' methods were being used to tranquillise prisoners.

In addition to the segregation areas in the main buildings, solitary confinement units under the old cow barn were viewed. These units consisted of five-by-seven-foot cells encased by heavy plexiglass, each installed within another bare cell and furnished only with a mattress, a bucket for toilet use, naked light bulbs burning twenty-four hours a day, and a vent no larger than a grapefruit. In these cells, daytime was distinguished by two sparse meals, and nighttime by two glasses of water. Although the 'cow barn' was ordered closed many years ago because of its primitive conditions, it continues to be used periodically to accommodate the overflow each time there is a disturbance.

The women's section, while smaller and less grim in its general appearance, produced even more complaints. "The clinic is a laugh," said one woman. "We get a hot two-minute interview, and that's called medical attention.... One doctor prescribes for withdrawal pains, the other won't." While there was a classroom, it had room for only six prisoners. Work programmes for the women fitted the traditional stereotypes: laundry, kitchen, and hairdressing, with pay ranging from 35¢ to $2.00 per day. One exception was the tailor shop, which provided excellent training, but according to Justice Patricia Proudfoot, "materials, staff and money were lacking."

Not only did the women have their solitary confinement unit in the basement, but they, too, were taken down the hill to the cow barn. Although in 1975 the Attorney-General had described it as a 'mind bomber' to be phased out within three weeks, in late November 1984 it was still there, and in use.

In 1975, I had been teaching a Women's Studies class at Oakalla. A month following the July sit-in at which I was among the group of prisoners' supporters, the class was cancelled and my teaching privileges and visiting rights withdrawn. Although no official reason was given, the Warden had learned of my participation in a demonstration protesting the death of Mary Steinhauser at the B.C. Pen in June. The B.C. Human

Rights Branch of the Department of Labour assisted in recovering my visiting rights, but it was a hollow victory since I was restricted to visiting the Doukhobour women prisoners.

Eight Doukhobour women were housed in a separate hut away from the prison population. Members of a religious sect, they were vegetarian pacifists who strongly believed in living and rearing their children according to their anti-militarist creed, which often conflicted with Canadian laws. Their way of protesting these laws was to set fires and disrobe. The Doukhobour women viewed their 'crimes' as minor compared with the son of a visiting official who was an officer in Vietnam at that time. "Your son is burning people," they told him. "We only burn our mattresses."

Some of the women, whose homes were in the interior of B.C., had been transferred to Kingston Prison for Women in Ontario. Understandably, they had been carrying out many protests, including a seven-month fast, and were very ill. One woman who was due for release refused to leave without her companion, who was sixty-three years old and still had six months to serve. The Prisoners' Rights Group (P.R.G.) initiated a campaign that succeeded in obtaining a Special Executive Clemency Order, and the two women were flown home to B.C. together.

As news spread about the P.R.G.'s involvement with the Doukhobour women, many prisoners wrote letters of praise and respect for them as fellow prisoners. Even the women in Kingston Prison, who had initially been quite hostile toward the Doukhobour women because they didn't understand their principles, began to leave vegetables by their cell doors as a gesture of support.

Although correspondence with the Administration was rarely satisfying, talking with the women after they came out of Oakalla was something else again. Like the men, the women had pasty complexions (too much starch in their diet and too little fresh air and sunshine), matched by their dull, bored attitude. But 'Mary' was different. She was keen to know what was going on in the outside world, and earnestly wanted to help break down the public apathy about prison life.

Some of 'Mary's' stories were amusing; others were not. One was about L.L., whose illness was ignored until she was rushed to hospital with intestinal obstruction and toxemia, and emergency surgery was performed. When she attended a Women's Studies class after her recovery, she showed us her scars. A few months later, L.L. hanged herself with her dressing gown belt.

'Mary' was anxious to expose Oakalla. As soon as she was released, contacts with the media were arranged.

On a radio programme in November 1977, 'Mary' described the brutality of the male guards: "...as soon as she sees a man she automatically cringes up... they don't just come in ones, they come in threes. It is going to be physical violence because there is no way... three guards and one girl." When asked if there was anything to the talk about sex between inmates and guards, she replied: "I have seen a male guard go into a woman's room after ten p.m. lock-up and stay in there for a while...." And about rehabilitation programmes: "There is none at all... we just sit around."

After the interview, 'Mary' told us that she would "sure have to watch [her] back. But it's worth it."

"Three days after the broadcast, 'Mary', 26, was found dead in a hotel room in Vancouver, apparently from a drug overdose" (*The Province*, November 21, 1977).

"Apparently from a drug overdose" is the way the media so often report the finding of dead bodies of ex-prisoners. No inquest. No police investigation. And the family more often than not are persuaded to authorise an immediate cremation.

Who is researching unreported, unresolved deaths of ex-prisoners?

In 1977, a Royal Commission of Inquiry into the Incarceration of Female Offenders was established, partly in response to a report presented by the Prisoners' Rights Group (P.R.G.) at a Citizens' Advisory Board meeting. The Inquiry dealt with sexual misconduct and demoralisation in the women's unit at Oakalla. After the shattering testimony from many witnesses, the Commission found that the prison was poorly run, and male guards were taking advantage of their position to intrude on the women's privacy. The Hearings concluded with fifty-seven recommendations, including barring male staff from certain areas and establishing meaningful educational and job-training programmes.

31

These recommendations, like the demands from the prisoners during the 1975 sit-in, were, for the most part, ignored.

Not surprisingly, on New Year's Eve 1979 the women at Oakalla again staged a sit-in, which developed into a small riot. Among other things, they were again protesting the presence of male guards, as well as cutbacks in medical, educational and visiting programmes. The fourteen 'leaders' of this incident were carted off to the supposedly 'phased out' cow barn, where they staged yet another protest. They refused to be released individually, demanding that they *all* be released together or none would move. The Administration finally had to concede.

And yet another investigation was extracted from the Attorney-General's Department "in response to an alarming number of reports of violent confrontations between guards and prisoners, of harsh and arbitrary use of discipline and a general atmosphere of tension and hostility" (*Vancouver Free Press*, January 18, 1980). Again, the same unhinged results....

The authorities at Oakalla continued to effectively bar the public from entering the prison. The media, too, unable to get 'hard' news, became apathetic and tended to discontinue their watchdog role.

In November 1983, Oakalla 'came down' — a full-blown riot in which rocks were thrown, fixtures ripped out, and cells and furniture smashed and burned. An eye-witness to the pattern of unrest, communication breakdown and harassment by guards which led to the riot described events following it:

> The handcuffs had been placed on... very tightly... hands were numb and the handcuffs had actually cut right into the skin, drawing blood.... We were driven to the cow barns... prodded inside... guards with their clubs pushed in our backs, pushing, sticking, swinging up between our legs from behind... beatings could be heard, the cracks on the head sounding clearly as well as blows to the body.
>
> ...bleeding as they were led to... total isolation. Several guards went... with them... the next morning, they were taken to the hospital, shaking violently and barely able to stand. (*Solidarity Times*, November 30, 1983)

The subsequent investigation had prison officials denying the mistreatment with the usual burlesque variations of:

> ...no excessive use of force, only calm, well-trained staff dealing with a very tense situation without harming prisoners. (*Solidarity Times*, November 30, 1983)

In late 1984, a rare success was scored by a well organised three-day fast to protest the poor quality and quantity of food provided by a private company under government contract. 'Privatisation', which actually increased the cost of food services by thirty to fifty per cent because of the need to build in a profit, was now extended to the prison system, abolishing the staff-run kitchen services. After this protest, the government was obliged to publicly warn the company about its practices. Weeks later, however, the success could be termed dubious, since the prisoners were again protesting the quality and quantity of meals.

There was a total of 639 attempted suicides by hanging, slashing, or other means at Oakalla between 1976 and 1978 (B.C. Corrections, 1984), which is hardly surprising when prisoners involved or even suspected of being involved in any kind of protest are confined in total isolation in cells with no heat, "years of blood and shit caked on [the walls, and] graffiti about death...." The riots, hostage-takings and escapes continue to take their toll of men and women doing 'hard time' at Oakalla, even as prison officials go on violating Gaol Rules and Regulations.

Having been effectively barred from visiting prisoners at Oakalla for no accountable reason since 1978, I have sought continuously through many avenues to have the order rescinded. Justice Proudfoot, in her Report on the Incarceration of Female Offenders (1977), had this to say:

> ...this Commission does not criticise the Corrections Director for taking this type of action if warranted. However, this Commission does condemn action such as this being taken without giving the individual affected an adequate explanation. Once again, officious action of this type can only bring the administration into disrepute. Ms. Culhane

is entitled to know why she is barred from O.W.C.C. [Oakalla Women's Correctional Centre].

In March 1978, a letter from the B.C. Corrections Director stated:

> Your visiting privileges at Oakalla have been discontinued until further notice. I have taken this decision because I believe that to continue your visiting privileges at this time would not be in the best interests of the institutions.

Again, no specific reasons were given. A month later, the Director, in a meeting with my lawyer, refused to give any details or reveal the circumstances upon which his decision was based, saying that to do so would affect the security of the institution.

A petition was then sought for an order reviewing, setting aside, or quashing the Director's decision to terminate my visits. It was brought on the grounds of a failure to comply with the rule of natural justice and the duty to act fairly, in that the decision-maker failed to provide the petitioner with notice of the factual allegations upon which the decision was made, and failed to provide an opportunity to the petitioner to respond to the allegations. On October 6, 1978, Mr. Justice G.G.S. Rae dismissed the petition, concluding that the nature of the decision was "purely administrative."

A petition of appeal was again filed with the B.C. Court of Appeals in 1979, requesting that the decision of the Regional Director to terminate my visiting rights at Oakalla be set aside. This appeal, too, was dismissed in January 1980, with one of three votes dissenting. Mr. Justice J. A. Lambert stated:

> The circumstances and the nature of the decision made by [the Regional Director] required that Ms. Culhane be informed of the allegations against her upon which the decision was based and that she be given an opportunity to answer them.

The next step, a prohibitively costly one, is to appeal to the Supreme Court of Canada, that is to say, if one is to rely solely on the Justice system.

I am not aware nor have I ever been advised of any facts or events which could reasonably lead to the conclusion that I am or have been a security risk to any prison. For the record, no obstacles have been placed in the way of my visiting in other provincial centres, to date.

If ordinary citizens on the 'outside' can be dealt with in this fashion — pronounced guilty with little or no recourse — it can be assumed that far more outrageous treatment does, in fact, occur on the 'inside.' The need to monitor the functioning of the rule of law inside prisons is therefore of paramount importance.

## B.C. Penitentiary

> The perverse logic of the law that visits the utmost limits of barbarity upon men admittedly guilty of minor transgressions. (Alexander Berkman)

In June 1975, three B.C. Pen prisoners held fifteen hostages for forty-one hours. The incident ended, if there ever is an end to such incidents, with the tactical squad moving in and firing on hostages and prisoners alike. Mary Steinhauser, a Classification Officer known for her empathy with the prisoners, was shot to death and one of the hostage-takers was seriously wounded. No charges were laid against the guards. This was not the first such episode at the B.C. Pen, nor was it to be the last:

**July 1975:** Prison barbering instructor held hostage eight hours by one prisoner.

**February 1976:** Two guards held for fifteen hours by two prisoners.

**April 1976:** Three guards held for thirteen hours by four prisoners. Two prisoners found dead.

**June 1976:** Attempt to take two guards hostage. They escape with minor injuries.

**August 1976:** One guard held hostage for ten minutes.

**September 1976:** Prisoner stabbed to death. A sex offender, he had been placed in general population despite warnings from prisoners to have him returned to the Protective Custody Unit (P.C.U.).

**September 1976:** Twelve-day state of emergency when guards refused to work overtime. Three prisoners dead.

*Six deaths in six months.*

In October 1976, the Commissioner of Penitentiaries had this to say: "...more than forty incidents over the last three years involving approximately 100 employees have been resolved without loss of life," ignoring the deaths of Mary Steinhauser and six prisoners.

*The Province* (March 19, 1976) headlined an article with "More Pen Violence Forecast":

> Rising tension in the segregation section of the B.C. Pen is bound to create new outbursts of violence.... prison has so far failed to meet any of the demands [such as] serving of meals by kitchen staff rather than guards to end what the inmates charged was contamination of food with cigarette butts and broken glass by vindictive guards, [and] lawyers not permitted to talk with segregation inmates although it had originally been planned for them to do so....

Journalist Allan Fotheringham added further insight into the situation with an article in *Maclean's* (October 18, 1976) entitled "Canada doesn't have to execute people any more, just sentence them to neglect."

> Since 1970 there have been 62 suicides. There is the disaster of the guards' situation. Underpaid, undertrained... they are even more cynical than the public. At the B.C. Pen the turnover rate among senior security people reached 75% to 80% in 1974. When they put on a crash programme to recruit and train new guards... they got fifty. Within two months half of them had quit.

Since hope is all a prisoner has, the warfare inside and suicide are bound to increase.... puzzling why we have to put more people in jail (per capita) than England, Denmark, Sweden, France, Italy, Japan, Spain, Norway and Holland.... It is remarkable that our prisons are now wiping out the reputation of Sing Sing and Alcatraz and are approaching Attica.

And, according to the P.S.A.C. (guards' union) (*Minutes of Proceedings*, November 1976):

...we have a motion on our books that we will not jeopardise the lives of any officer, that we have the power to take whatever action we... deem necessary... *We can and will run the institution*, and if this means keeping them locked up, this is what will happen. (Emphasis added)

A letter signed by over 200 B.C. Pen prisoners dated September 14, 1976, was sent to the *Vancouver Sun*, with these suggestions:

Move Security (P.S.A.C.) beyond the fence and issue them whatever weaponry they feel necessary to prevent our escape into society's ranks. Issue each of them a *tank* if necessary, but move them out of the inner operations of the institution. In that way, (1) they would not be exposed to the 'danger' they claim exists; (2) the massive overtime they now work, amounting to millions of dollars annually across Canada, would bring big savings to the public; and (3) the turmoil so necessary to justify the strengthening of their union would quickly disappear, to the public's satisfaction.

Sometime during the third week of September, the Inmate Committee (I.C.) handed notes to two shifts of guards, begging them to sit down and parley in an attempt to diffuse the explosive situation. The Committee was convinced that many would have done so had they not feared intimidation by the 'heavies' in their union. The I.C. also informed the Warden that two of the main demands of the guards' union were to cut back on recreation and social activities, and to increase lock-up time. This was followed by a press release in which the prisoners stated that "...the twenty-four P.S.A.C. demands were not negotiable [and] gave conditions that could only result in a riot."

"The B.C. Pen 'Comes Down'," screamed a newspaper headline of September 27, 1976.

- 25 of the 95 cells in the North wing were wrecked.
- 50 of the 110 cells in B-7 were gone.
- 200 cells in the East block were almost totally destroyed.
- 2 hostages were being held in the kitchen area.

The Pen quickly took on the appearance of an armed fortification. Fifty army combat troops patrolled the perimeter. Joined by the R.C.M.P. and the New Westminster police, the security guards were well reinforced.

"We did in twelve hours what the Federal government couldn't do in fifty years," the prisoners taunted. They had a point. No one could dispute the official directives over the last *thirty* years ordering the 'phasing out of the B.C. Pen.'

From the outside, clanging and shouting rang from the East Block. Ten bedsheets were strung along ten smashed windows reading: SOLIDARITY. Significantly, this slogan was never reported or photographed in any media throughout the disturbance.

On the inside, the end product of the wrecking spree in the East wing — a mass of torn mattresses, splintered bookcases and cupboards, smashed sinks and toilets, and two sheets hung on the bars, spelling UNDER NEW MANAGEMENT.

Except for the Protective Custody Unit, where those convicted of sex offences and those labelled 'informers' did their time, and the Super Maximum Security Unit (S.M.S.U. — the solitary confinement area), the prisoners, represented by their Inmate Committee (I.C.), had taken over the 'joint'.

Their first demand — that the Citizens' Advisory Committee (C.A.C.) be called in as observers — was clearly intended to reduce any likelihood of a tragic repetition of the 1975 hostage-taking incident in which Mary Steinhauser had been killed and a prisoner seriously wounded.

In a paper prepared shortly before the events of September 1976, the I.C. had stated that "The power struggle between B.C. Pen Custody and all other departments was at its peak and we were let know that we were treading on dangerous ground...." This attitude on behalf of the guards had been generated by a combination of factors. Negotiation time for their union had once again arrived. A pattern of unrest provided a useful background for their demands for increased pay, shorter hours, and earlier retirement. And with yet another 'riot' to contend with, 'hard pressed,' 'overworked' and 'underpaid' guards could expect to garner support from the public.

As the prisoners were being 'allowed' to smash up their cells for three days, the I.C. felt compelled, understandably, to expose what was to them by now a familiar strategy. Contrary to some interpretations, there are occasions when prisoners deliberately stage a hostage-taking in an attempt to *avert* violence rather than to *create* it. The September 27th action was such an occasion, initiated in order to halt the growing momentum and to forestall the guards from using their clubs and tear gas; to inform the public so that everyone could see that it was not just another case of prisoners acting out their stereotyped 'violent and irresponsible' role; and to bring in the C.A.C. This was to be the first opportunity for a group of citizens to actively participate in a confrontation between prisoners and the Administration *during an actual crisis*. In the words of one of the hostage-takers:

> The riot was simmering for the better part of three days. Not one thing was done by the Administration to curb the impending riot or to alleviate the tensions. The only party trying to get things back to an even keel was the Inmate Committee who were met with opposition and open hostility by the Administration at every turn. We were made to understand that Custody was in the process of getting ready to rush the East wing with tear gas and clubs to subdue the rioters. We knew there was also the possibility of great loss of life to our brothers because many of them were quite prepared to die for their cause. Things had deteriorated too far to hope for a peaceful settlement, *so when we were asked to take hostages, we did*

*because it was the only thing to do.* (Court transcript, April 25, 1977) (Emphasis added)

The I.C. demanded a press conference in order to make the public aware of what was going on. As a show of good faith, they released one of the two hostages during the conference. Their initial press release had included, in part:

> The Inmate Committee wants it made public how this incident came about and to expose the corruption of this institution. No demands to escape have been made by anyone.... The cause of this incident lies other than with the prisoners, and we want to prove this to the public....
>
> Every attempt made by the Inmate Committee over the past two months [including] a letter-writing campaign with over 100 letters [and] appeals and telegrams to Ottawa... met with deaf ears.
>
> This Penitentiary is not so much the problem as it is the result of a grotesque justice and court system. Prisoners are being used as political pawns by selfishly-motivated politicians who don't really care about the consequences.

At the press conference, the I.C. presented an interim statement: "While there are many other needs, immediate and urgent, the Inmate Committee is endeavouring to maintain an attitude of reasonable negotiations in order to expedite the release of the hostages, and the transfer of prisoners. It is hoped that this change will serve as a basis for improved conditions." The clauses covered key matters such as reprisals, voluntary transfers, personal possessions to be returned intact, Super Maximum Security Unit (solitary), approved transfers, status of the Inmate Committee, and most important of all — a public inquiry.

It became clear that had the media come in two days earlier, the riot may not have happened. Negotiations could have begun, and perhaps some significant compromises might have been reached once the public became aware of the gravity of what was taking place inside.

During the time negotiations were underway, there remained one area in which the Administration was successful in undermining the I.C.'s intentions. Although the I.C. had been agitating constantly for a representative, accompanied by members of the C.A.C., to be allowed to visit their brothers in S.M.S.U., the Administration could and did prevent them from doing so. After some argument, this demand was reluctantly granted.

The general population was equally concerned. Rumours were filtering down that all was not well in the 'Penthouse,' as the S.M.S.U. was known.

It was agreed that only male members of the C.A.C. would join the I.C. as they travelled through the prison, since it could reasonably be considered an invasion of privacy if women went into areas where toilets and showers were open to view. Ironically, since that time female guards are proliferating through the prison system, and male prisoners are trying to take the Correctional Service of Canada (C.S.C.) to court to keep women guards out of the areas where they use the toilets and showers, and from being present during strip searches. They have been informed "...that the searching of male inmates by female staff is seen as socially acceptable whereas the converse (male staff searching female prisoners) is not true" (*Globe & Mail*, October 19, 1984).

After a brief trip upstairs, the C.A.C. and I.C. reported that they found several inches of water on cell floors and that the prisoners were in their underwear or nude. An excerpt from a prisoner's letter tells us:

> The screws took all their anger out on us up here cuz they couldn't do it to the rest of the guys in population. They brought the fire hose on the range every couple of hours to flood our cells out, laughing while they did it. We all got skin frisks [strip naked, bend over, spread cheeks] and all our clothes and bedding taken away. I managed to keep a few things dry for I could hear them start at cell number 1 with the fire hose and I'm in number 10. This kept up for three days....
>
> The nurse came up here once and seen everyone in their cells with no clothes, bedding, cells flooded. She didn't do fuck all about it. No doctor's been up, no medication.... The screws turned the heat off and opened all the windows too. The lights are on twenty-four hours a

day now. The only thing I want is a hot shower, dry clothes, dry bedding....

Although the C.A.C. had the authority, by virtue of the *Letter of Understanding* with the C.P.S. (Sec. 4, Clause F), "to inform the public... of issues arising within the institution," it refused to do so, despite the insistence of one of its members.

When the time came to move prisoners out of the smashed East wing, the I.C. requested that the R.C.M.P. be brought in. They preferred to have an outside force around, instead of the guards who could be expected to take their revenge when the observers had left. Later, when two R.C.M.P. officers informally queried this request, an I.C. member offered to introduce them to two prisoners "whose brains are now scrambled," who had survived a similar riot at Millhaven Penitentiary the previous year. They had had to run the gauntlet of two rows of guards with clubs as they were moved naked from the yard on their hands and knees back to their cells. "By bringing in outside police this time, we just figured we would try and avoid having that happen here," it was explained.

The delay in finalising the negotiations was partly due to the many postponements, some of them at the request of the I.C. as they rushed to different areas of the prison to deal with minor crises. Men had been living in a cold, miserable garbage heap for almost a week now, and there were bound to be some who couldn't take the endless strain, especially when they learned how the Administration was up to its usual delaying tactics.

It wasn't long before the first attempt was made to oust the C.A.C. On September 30, a phone call was received warning the C.A.C. to leave the gym immediately, inferring that the situation was getting out of hand and that they would be in danger. But the C.A.C. insisted on remaining pending further clarification of the 'evacuation instructions.' No further order came through.

The following day, by coincidence, it was reported in the local newspaper that "the prison authorities planned to tear gas those rebellious prisoners... but then called it off" (*Columbian*, October 1, 1976).

And again, just hours before the signing of the Memorandum of Agreement, the C.A.C. was offered the opportunity to leave the gym 'before Security moved in.' They refused. And again nothing happened.

The Memorandum of Agreement defined itself as "the basis upon which the management of the B.C. Pen, the I.C. and the C.A.C. agreed to end the current situation within the penitentiary," and was dealt with as follows:

**1.** *Mr. Culbert, who is being held in the kitchen of the Penitentiary, will be released unharmed immediately.*

Mr. Culbert was released unharmed immediately after the Memorandum was signed.

**2.** *a) The inmates with Mr. Culbert will turn themselves over to the R.C.M.P. who will have complete responsibility for their safe removal to an R.C.M.P. lockup and transfer to another Federal Penitentiary.*

While they did turn themselves over to the R.C.M.P. and were transferred to other federal penitentiaries, the story did not end there. See items 4 (a) and (c).

*b) The R.C.M.P. will take complete responsibility for the safe removal of men from the damaged area of the Penitentiary. In performing this role, the R.C.M.P. will be observed by members of the Citizens' Advisory Committee and the Inmate Committee.*

The transfer out of the smashed areas and later out of the crowded gym was uppermost in every prisoner's mind. Some 240 had been held in the gym for over a month, and it was almost two months after the Agreement was signed before the final fifty prisoners were evacuated from the gym, and then only because of a fire. Conditions had been deplorable: lack of medical care; frequent slashings and suicide threats; filthy living conditions; inadequate food and hygiene facilities; no recreation or visitors. In short, once again a potentially dangerous atmosphere had been created. Tensions ran extremely high between prison staff and prisoners, and it was hoped that the R.C.M.P. involvement would act as a buffer between the two.

> *c) The R.C.M.P. will take total responsibility for the transfer of all inmates.*

This was to ensure that nothing would happen in transit. It was already known that prisoners were being beaten en route, or were being delivered to unscheduled destinations.

> *d) The R.C.M.P. will remain within the B.C. Pen for a period of two weeks and after the first week will meet with management, the Inmate Committee and the Citizens' Advisory Committee to discuss any [further] need for their presence.*

However, within one week the Administration, acting unilaterally, dismissed the R.C.M.P., leaving one token officer on duty. Then, on the excuse that there wasn't sufficient supervisory staff, for the next two months prisoners were deprived of the exercise yard.

### 3. Transfers
*a) All inmates within uninhabitable areas of the penitentiary will immediately be removed to habitable areas... and receive necessary medical attention.*

This clause was violated from the moment the Agreement was signed. In addition to the conditions in the gym, which were becoming unbearable, 'necessary medical attention', for the most part, was non-existent, and when it did exist, it was inadequate, often life-threatening, despite the Penitentiary Regulation which states: "Every inmate shall be provided in accordance with directives, with the essential medical and dental care that he requires."

Excerpts from the Prisoners' Log attest to how this clause was violated:

> *Oct. 15* — Have been trying to get emergency dental treatment for Tom L. for four consecutive days. The hospital has insisted on sending [only] oil of cloves.... the

tooth is broken almost to the gum and the nerve is completely exposed.... Tom is in such pain that he is threatening to rip the tooth out of his own mouth.

*Oct. 22* — ...problems getting medical attention for Joseph E. who has internal bleeding and lengthy medical trauma. In fact, he is dying.... Joseph E. went to the hospital after the Committee telephoned many times and finally got results.

*Oct. 24* — Joseph E. states that his symptoms make him aware that he requires blood transfusions for his condition. He is having problems getting to hospital as attending nurse in gym states it's not time for his transfusion even though, by date, he is past due. The nurse has taken it on her own to deny him medical aid and overrule the doctor's duties.

*Oct. 31* — Bob S. has been out of crutches a very short time [after] many operations and marrow replacement... pain unbearable... obviously requires medication... He politely requested that she [nurse] go back to the hospital and check his medical file. She gave a definite NO to him, refused to discuss it or check his file....

*Nov. 14* — Clarence P. just slashed.

*b) Every case of an inmate requesting voluntary transfer from the B.C. Pen will be referred for decision to a Committee consisting of the Regional Transfer Board and the Citizens' Advisory Committee.*

Voluntary transfer from the B.C. Pen, particularly for those who were in the gym, was one of the most urgent issues. With the C.A.C. working with the Transfer Board for the first time, the prisoners were especially encouraged. They had been accustomed to being moved without any opportunity to present their cases.

However, when the C.A.C. realised that it was being permitted only to 'observe' at Transfer Board hearings and would have no decision-making input, it stopped attending.

*c) All transfers will be to equivalent security in the institution to which the transfer is made.*

Nor was this clause honoured. Stories, and in some cases the men themselves, came back from other prisons where they had been placed in solitary confinement.

### 4. Reprisals

*a) There will be no physical punishment of any inmate involved in the incident.*

Countless examples demonstrate how this clause was abandoned. For instance, when transferred to other federal prisons, the hostage-takers were immediately placed in solitary confinement. And within three months of signing the Agreement, an I.C. member was severely beaten as he resisted removal to 'the hole' by the goon squad.

In addition to physical punishment, there were many incidents of harassment and intimidation. Again, from the Prisoners' Log:

> *Nov. 8* — Guard CX-2, known as hating inmates, after threatening to kill a member of the Committee... was placed right at the gym entrance where he can curse and heckle....
>
> *Nov. 14* — Guard in the cage had cocked a rifle three times and had called out B.'s name, which immediately brought screams and curses from below. [He was] leaning up against the opened cage window (as close as he could get to the inmates) smiling down on them....

*b) There will be no internal disciplinary charges laid until after consideration of the report of the public inquiry.*

Completely disregarding this clause, prisoners were put in solitary confinement immediately after they were transferred from the gym.

*c) No double jeopardy. If criminal charges are laid arising from the disturbance, no internal charges will be laid.*

The hostage-takers were kept in solitary confinement until they went to trial in April 1977, and for another three months afterwards — nine months in all — clearly a case of 'double jeopardy.'

### 5. Possessions
*All inmates, upon transfer, will be permitted to take with them personal effects, intact.*

Breach of this clause was common. For example, one prisoner's family photo album, supposedly 'lost', was discovered in the garbage with every picture torn up.

### 6. Super Maximum Unit
*Members of the Inmate Committee will be permitted to meet any inmates held in the Super Maximum Unit whom they request to see, or who requests to see them.*

The I.C. continued to be blocked from taking any effective action to relieve the paranoia, the 'insanity, the fear, the violence' which characterises solitary confinement.

### 7. Public Enquiry
*The Citizens' Advisory Committee recommends that the enquiry be full and open with broad terms of reference to enquire into the particular and general causes of the disturbance at the B.C. Pen, the resolution of the demands made by the inmates, the implementation of the settlement and the future role of the B.C. Pen in the prison system. The enquiry should be by an impartial person with the report of the enquiry to be released to the public.*

The Solicitor-General called for a subcommittee to carry out an inquiry, but their mandate was limited to an examination of the prison system in general, instead of relating the B.C. Pen emergency to the general crisis which characterises the Canadian Penitentiary Service. Resolution, implementation and settlement of the I.C.'s demands were never taken seriously. The future role of the B.C. Pen was defined by the 1978 Administration as able to last 'another 100 years.'

**8.** *It has been agreed that further meetings between the Management of the B.C. Penitentiary, the Inmate Committee, and the Citizens' Advisory Committee will continue, to discuss outstanding matters.*

47

No such further meetings took place. I.C. members were intimidated. The C.A.C., after manipulating the resignation of one of its most vocal members, evolved into a group recommended by the John Howard Society.

> **9.** *The Inmate Committee, as presently constituted, will stay in existence until another Inmate Committee is duly elected.*

The election of another Inmate Committee was postponed pending the Hearings of the Parliamentary Subcommittee so that the I.C. present during the 1976 crisis could testify. Shortly afterwards, all I.C. members but one were transferred to other parts of the country. It was not until 1979 that other prisoners, reluctant to step into the breach, stood for election. Those who ran did so only after approval from Security.

The Memorandum of Agreement was signed in good faith by the I.C. and the C.A.C. The last hostage was released, and the riot was over. Early on the morning of October 2, the C.A.C. walked out.

Three days later a letter arrived from the Commissioner declaring that the Agreement was devoid of legal effect:

> ...it is entirely a matter of Canadian Penitentiary Service discretion as to whether the so-called Agreement is to be honoured in full or in part, or at all.

Once again, the prisoners and the public had been deceived.

Nonetheless, this was the first time in the history of the Canadian Penitentiary Service that prisoners confronted the authorities with an outside group bearing witness from beginning to end. The Agreement was negotiated sincerely by a group of prisoners who had set out to improve conditions with the full realisation that they would be in the front line when the reprisals began.

In lieu of a public or judicial inquiry advocated by the Memorandum of Agreement, an all-party Parliamentary Subcommittee was commissioned by Parliament in 1977 to conduct a national investigation into the prison system. When it reached B.C., representatives of both the prisoners and the C.A.C. at the B.C. Pen offered insights and recommendations. To name just a few:

*From the C.A.C.:*
> As a basic principle that negotiation replace confrontation as the politics of prison;
>
> Within limitations, that inmates be given far greater responsibility for the conditions under which they must serve their sentence... using Inmate Committees in greater degree than they are at present;
>
> An Independent Chairperson to replace the Warden, for the Internal Disciplinary Board.

At a later period when this position was installed, questions arose as to what actual degree of independence existed when the person was appointed by the C.S.C., and in fact several have since resigned from the position because of this uncomfortable discrepancy.

*From the prisoners:*
> We are expected to learn in here how to live under social norms on the street. Unless there are social norms exercised in here we can never learn what they are... if we can discover that in here, maybe we can cope [when released];
>
> In 1974, I started a writing club... operated for six months. Two books were published by about thirty people, who may never have known they had the talent;
>
> There are some serious things [still] happening in this institution, and unless they change, there is going to be trouble again.

It was not long before that prediction came true.

Two years later, on January 28, 1978, six prisoners armed with firearms and knives held thirteen hostages in an apparent escape attempt, in the Visiting and Correspondence area. Their lawyer was refused access to her clients until they either surrendered or were arrested, and when she requested that the R.C.M.P. speak with the hostage-takers, they refused. She resigned.

Flowing from this incident, two of the hostages, women prison activists who had been among the visitors at the Pen that morning, were indicted on charges of complicity in the escape attempt. Despite the findings of a lengthy preliminary inquiry which dismissed all charges, the prosecutor decided to take them to trial by direct indictment, which completely nullified the earlier decision.

During the lengthy court procedure in which it was revealed that the hostage-takers had spent years in solitary confinement, the central issue was whether prisoners have a right (or an obligation) to attempt to escape from solitary confinement, which, by definition, is cruel and unusual punishment.

On March 21, 1979, the two women were acquitted.

By this time, the long-awaited phasing out of the B.C. Pen was underway. May 10, 1980 — the big day — featured some extraordinary speeches. The Solicitor-General described "our society's responsibility to make every effort to [continue] providing opportunities to offenders," and the newly appointed C.S.C. Commissioner wondrously proclaimed that "as this penitentiary is closed, it is time to remember that the institution has been at the forefront of progress."

A shiny souvenir brochure hoped that "...other new institutions will serve society as well as 'the Pen' did in its day."

Some time before the Pen's closure, a prisoner wrote to a Vancouver newspaper complaining about the mice and birds. "The birds zoom in and out of broken windows, leaving droppings splattered all over the cell block, and mice zip about squeaking and squealing at all hours of the night." He asked whether the mice and birds were a legal part of the judge's sentence. Having spotted a two-headed mouse, he wanted to know if the mouse would benefit science, and if so, to whom should he send it.

The decision to demolish the B.C. Pen was the final answer to that riddle.


## Dorchester

> Violence and tension between prisoners is encouraged by prison managers as a tool to control and distract prisoners from the conditions of their confinement. (Coalition for Prisoners' Rights, Santa Fe)

The lead story in the *Evening Patriot* on October 8, 1980, reads: "Three convicted murderers at the Dorchester Federal

Penitentiary took two guards hostage early today. Prison authorities said the only demands so far were for food and drugs, and attempts were being made to maintain communication with the hostage-takers...." Contrary to popular opinion, violence, let alone death, is rare in prisoner hostage-takings. The *Moncton Transcript* informs us that "Of the 70 [incidents] since 1974, 18 of the 212 [hostages] taken were slightly injured, and only 2 killed — both shot by tactical squad guards."

Three days later, the *Charlottetown Guardian* reported that the prisoners "...appeared to have been treating their captives well. However, during rescue operations by fellow guards, one of the 2 guards was killed by a shotgun blast from the [Institutional] Emergency Response Team [I.E.R.T.]" and that "the three prisoners were also injured."

Once more, loss of life occurred on prison grounds. But when an analytic search for an answer to this useless killing was sought, the Solicitor-General remained adamant as he continued to call for special jails. "The most secure prison is the one where prisoners spend most of their time in cells," he told the *Whig Standard* after the incident. The prisoners at Dorchester had, in fact, been confined to their cells since an escape attempt two months earlier.

There had been ample opportunity to avert the tragedy that occurred at this Maximum Security prison situated in a country setting about twenty-five miles from Moncton, New Brunswick. One approaches Dorchester along a winding road flanked by a farm on one side and a cemetery on the other. The scene contrasts sharply with the evident reality inside this ancient structure which resembles the B.C. Pen.

Prior to the hostage-taking, with a regularity bordering on futility, numerous attempts had been made by the prisoners to warn the Administration, and anyone else who would listen, of the potential for revolt. Once again, the warnings were either stifled or ignored. One such communication dated September 20, 1980, did reach me. It read:

> This letter has gone out the back door because, as you know, it would never get past the front. Dorchester is about to riot any time now. Prisoners are being put in the hole for no other reason but suspicion. Over half the

general population is in segregation now. They are hand-cuffed, taken off the range, thrown or pushed downstairs, and once in the hole they are beat by four, five, or six pigs, then gassed and shackled and left that way for days on end.

The brutality here is unreal. One guy was taken out of his cell, stripped, had his hands cuffed behind his back, and was told to lay face down on the cold cement while guards spent an hour searching his cell. Another was gassed in the hole because he told guards to lay off when they were beating another guy. Guards refused to take cuffs off another guy so he could eat his meals. He had to put his face in the tray so he could eat. Finally, he broke his handcuffs somehow after three or four days of pissing himself. Guards told him they run this prison now and they can do what they want with us.

Could you see about getting us some publicity? I'm working at this end along with the others. We have late radio stations and newspapers alerted, and are hoping for a good outcome. We need all the support we can get.

Official reaction to the publicity startled no one. From the Commissioner, quoted in the *Whig Standard*, October 23, 1980: "...letter was sensational but unnecessary. There are many channels for prisoners to seek redress for real or imagined inequities or brutalities.... With all these avenues it seems absurdly unnecessary to engage in the colourful charade of smuggling secret messages." And the Solicitor-General told the *Whig Standard* that the letter "gives the impression that inmates are suppressed, when they are not."

Following persistent appeals from prisoners as their visiting rights with families, lawyers and media were being cancelled, and finally when an agitated phone call was received from a prisoner just released from Dorchester, I felt compelled to travel to the trouble spot. Upon being denied access to the prisoners with whom I had been corresponding for some time, a two-day vigil at the prison gates helped publicise the need for an immediate investigation into the aftermath of the riot. Members of Parliament were urged to utilise their privileged status which granted them entry. It is worth noting that when prisoners clamour for public exposure and communication with outside functionaries, and are consistently denied, it should be evident that the burden of proof rests with those who have the power to authorise such meetings but refuse to do so.

The call for a full, judicial, open inquiry into the Dorchester affair was once again substituted with an assignment to the Inspector-General to conduct his own private investigation, which would then remain the property of the Solicitor-General's Ministry. However, when the N.D.P. critic was able to refer to the Report in the House of Commons on December 15, 1980, with complete accuracy (having received a copy through unknown channels), the Solicitor-General, undoubtedly with much distaste, tabled it for public debate.

Certain disclosures in the Report more than substantiated the prisoners' charges even as the effects were being downplayed. From the Report's eight findings, the following are of particular interest:

> When an inmate did not respond immediately, he was maced. An officer would grab the inmate's hands and pull on them to get them far enough out [through the bars], then cuff the wrists together. [While] four inmates complained of guards 'jumping up and down' on their hands... there were no observations made by the medical staff of any injuries at all to the top of the hands. In an interview with the Health Care Officer... it was confirmed that most inmates had numb, swolled, discoloured hands, more consistent with lack of circulation than a beating.
>
> The Board has little doubt that a few discreet shots of mace were applied unnecessarily despite the presence of R.C.M.P. officers. There is little doubt that some inmates were kicked on the hands or had them struck by a night stick, but the lack of physical injury indicated that these incidents were few and of *low intensity*. None of the fourteen inmates suffered any serious physical injuries.
>
> ...while the Board cannot condone rough and unprofessional behaviour on the part of the staff, it can easily understand it would have occurred. (Emphasis added)

Despite the fact that the Report states that the force used was "not excessive," it does agree that "It is generally recognised that the avoidance of detection is a major factor in crime," and they can "easily see that if an officer knows he cannot be identified then he can easily succumb to the temptation of hitting a bit harder or a few more times than is necessary."

Only one recommendation was made: *As a result of the foregoing findings, the Board recommends that Institutional Emergency Response Team members in all institutions be required to wear conspicuously displayed identification numbers.*

Incredible as it may appear, within a month of the Report being made public, thirty-eight prisoners were again sending out an S.O.S. — a signed petition dated January 31, 1981, sent to me to be forwarded to the Solicitor-General. As usual, this petition was widely circulated by the Prisoners' Rights Group (P.R.G.). It read, in part:

> We, the undersigned, once again are attempting to bring to the attention and enlighten the public of the frustrating, inhumane treatment and conditions we are forced to live under here in the segregation unit... for the past three and a half months.
>
> We, the inmates here in segregation, through the proper grievance procedure, have filed more than 100 complaints in the past three months to no avail. Although these complaints have been answered in writing, the Warden has done nothing to rectify these problems.... Until now we have done nothing to protest these conditions. We have tolerated this unjust treatment in hope that there may yet be an independent inquiry into this corrupt institution that could possibly reveal the truth of some of the incompetent, irresponsible people who are in charge.
>
> We ask you to attempt to have these very serious conditions rectified, as we cannot tolerate the responsible people who are *not* attempting to rectify the situation.

On receipt of his copy, Svend Robinson, N.D.P. M.P., despatched his own letter to the Solicitor-General expressing his anxiety about the allegations made:

> ...concerning the continuing segregation of prisoners, the intransigence of the Administration in refusing to meet with the Inmate Committee and the apparent violation

of regulations concerning the opening of privileged mail. I am very concerned that the harsh measures still being imposed on Dorchester's inmates could lead to further problems or incidents, and I would urge that you instruct your officials to accord prisoners at least those minimal rights to hygiene and recreation that they are entitled to.

Obviously the rule of law doesn't have any part to play in the prisons of the country.

The tensions outlined in the Inspector-General's report on Dorchester Penitentiary continued to escalate. In the five-year period from 1978 to 1982, there were four suicides in Atlantic Region prisons. When the number of suicides in the first quarter of 1983 reached seven, the Solicitor-General commissioned yet another inquiry. A study headed by Dr. E. H. Botterell produced startling data.

From 1977 to 1982, the suicide rate in the Atlantic Region was 73.4 per 100,000, significantly lower than the rest of the country, which was 103.3 per 100,000. However, in the first quarter of 1983, the Atlantic rate soared to 78.5 per 100,000, which the study group described as a "statistically significant increase."

In comparing the frequency of suicides in the general population of Canada with those in prisons, the study calculated that the rate in Canada was 27.6 per 100,000 per year, whereas the rate in penitentiaries between January 1977 and September 1983 was 111.3 per 100,000. Thus there were seventy-five suicides in prisons compared to approximately nineteen per year on the outside.

The correlation between the increase in the prison population and the higher suicide rate demonstrated an increase in suicides of 14.8% in the Atlantic Region, matched by 7.9% in the penitentiary system as a whole. For the same time period, the prison population in the Atlantic Region increased by 40.7% compared with 21.6% for the rest of Canada, and the population of Dorchester increased by 52% compared with 22.5% for all maximum security prisons throughout Canada.

These statistics must be viewed in the light of an atmosphere in which medical personnel are "about 100 medicals [examinations] behind" schedule; where responses to grievances "are so slow as to be, in many cases, meaningless"; where psychiatrists are so overloaded that they have little time for patient-inmates; and where Case Management Officers admit that "while the newcomer is required to be seen within five days of arrival, it is frequently more than three months before they are personally counselled."

Such a level of inefficiency broadens the scope of possible criminality in the handling of health care for prisoners. For example, the Study included Inmate Committee concerns that "the nursing staff changes patient-inmates' medication without the doctor's orders," and that "inmates are prescribed medication that is not used for the public." While the Study Team felt that these practices were extremely unlikely, the use of prisoner 'volunteers' as subjects of experimentation for large-scale medical research is becoming all too common, a fact which must be exposed and halted.

The Nuremberg Judgement has ruled:

> Voluntary consent... is absolutely essential... that the person... should have the legal capacity to give consent [and] be so situated as to be able to exercise free power of choice.... should have sufficient knowledge and comprehension of the elements of the subject matter involved so as to enable... understanding, enlightened decisions.

Current prison conditions obviously do not provide such preconditions. Prisons in Canada serve the purpose *as they are*. Quoted in *Kind and Usual Punishment*, an official at Wyeth Laboratories revealed that "Almost all our Phase 1 testing is done in prisons... if prisons closed down tomorrow the pharmaceutical companies would be in one hell of a bind."

The Study on Atlantic Suicides did recognise that "more problem people [are] coming into C.S.C. because of the cutbacks in the community mental hospitals." Recognition must also be given to the correlation between the diminishing opportunities for the 15- to 29-year-old age group and the increase in the prison population of that group, which now forms the majority of prisoners in Canada. In any analysis of the Canadian prison system, this issue must be given a high priority.

# Matsqui

> A large community of prison officials and others has a
> vested interest in the present power structure and would
> be opposed to reform of any kind from any source. (Dr.
> Karl Menninger)

Before Matsqui was opened in 1966, it was touted as a
model treatment centre for criminal drug addicts. It was to
be one of five Canadian treatment centres, housing 312 male
and 128 female addicts in a pleasant setting about forty-five
miles from Vancouver in the Fraser Valley. The hospital-like
institution was to be associated with the University of British
Columbia, but under Canadian Penitentiary Service jurisdiction.

By 1972, much to the disappointment of those who needed
its services, it was transformed into a male Medium Security
prison. The pilot drug treatment programme had been phased
out (to the relief of many who saw it as almost sadistic) with
the emphasis now on regular offenders. Perhaps this was, in
part, in anticipation of accommodating prisoners from the
B.C. Pen, which was to eventually be dismantled.

Prisoners who had been transferred to Matsqui from other
prisons at an earlier period were quoted as saying that the
main difference they experienced was the lack of violence compared with other prisons. Although there had not been any
*major* disturbances, there were a number of episodes in which
prisoners protested over specific grievances.

National Prison Justice Day, August 10, has been set aside
each year since 1976. Prisoners and supporters gather to respect
the memory of those who have died unnatural deaths in Canadian prisons. In 1978, the men at Matsqui participated in
their usual peaceful, non-violent manner with a twenty-four-
hour fast and work stoppage, as did approximately 3,500 others
throughout Canada. Prior to the event, as was their custom,
the Prisoners' Rights Group (P.R.G.) had contacted prison
officials requesting confirmation that no reprisals would take
place either inside or outside prison walls, meaning that friends
and relatives who participated would not have their visiting
rights cut off. Most other prison officials responded favourably.
Matsqui, however, chose to punish the prisoners by cancelling

their monthly open house family day, as well as other social events for a period of one month.

Over the years, August 10th has been marked by a show of exceptional solidarity. As a result of the large number of transfers, both voluntary and involuntary, there is always some prisoner present to keep its meaning alive and to explain to newcomers its significance. Fasts and work stoppages continue to take place in most prisons — sometimes by just a handful, but other times with 100% participation. August 10th also provides families and supporters with a place and time to meet each year to hold vigils, demonstrations, marches, street theatre and, in some cities, church services. It is our way of keeping the public informed about the many injustices they would not otherwise hear about.

By 1984, there were reports from the U.S., France and Belgium that some prisoners and their supporters were participating in the Canadian National Prison Justice Day. Similarly, September 13th and February 2nd have become known as Attica Day and Santa Fe Day, not only to recall the barbarism of the bloody riots on those dates, but also to draw attention to the fact that conditions have not improved anywhere on the prison scene. Regardless of the number in attendance, the day holds a deep significance to the many who press for abolition of prisons (see Appendix I).

From 1975 to 1981, prisoners at Matsqui had produced a highly successful theatre programme. The first of its kind, it received standing ovations and favourable reviews over the years. Its plays included such classics as *Three Penny Opera*, *The Caretaker*, and *The Homecoming*. Initially described as a "socialisation experiment," it had, by 1981, evolved into an independently funded society managed solely by the prisoners themselves. During its six years of operation, some 367 male prisoners and thirteen volunteer female actors were involved. The Acting Warden at that time said of the programme: "During the period that the plays are going on, there is a type of self-control exhibited where they tend to assist one another to keep out of trouble" (*Interface*, June 1981). The last play performed, *Boss Ubu*, had two prisoners deferring their release dates in order to participate.

Despite such uplifting interludes, the propensity for trouble is never far from the surface. A few months later, headlines sensationalised: "Much of Matsqui damaged — prison rioters give up." Approximately 300 prisoners had taken control of the building for several hours, smashing furniture and setting fire to much of the prison. There were no attempted escapes, no hostage-takings, and the prisoners took the time to warn some nurses before the riot took place.

By the next morning, some 200 R.C.M.P. officers, 180 army troops, twenty Matsqui police officers, six dogs and fourteen ambulances had been called out in an incredible show of force. Rifles, shotguns, clubs and other riot gear were well displayed. The prisoners surrendered, but not without incident.

According to prison officials, warning shots were fired on several occasions, but no shots were aimed directly at prisoners. However, one prisoner required hospital treatment for pellet wounds to his face, shoulder and arm. This was further substantiated by a guard who had been involved in the riot. In an anonymous interview with *The Province* (June 5, 1981), the guard said, "It's garbage that no one was shot at," and that guards purposely shot at prisoners, including the one now in hospital. In another incident, guards pumped from seven to ten shotgun shots into a building containing some prisoners to force them to clear the building. "We were equipped with heavy gauge shotguns and AR-15 rifles that could stop a truck," he said. But they were forbidden to use tear gas.

The riot was apparently triggered by working conditions in the kitchen, although the Mandatory Supervision system and changes in the pay system were thought to be major predisposing factors overall. The prisoners were able to give their version of the riot two days after the event when four of them flagged down reporters who were about to leave the prison.

The press corps had been told that the prisoners' spokesmen had failed to show up at a previously arranged press conference. However, when the four prisoners held up a sign that read PRESS NEEDED, URGENT, NO VIOLENCE, and were then asked why they didn't appear earlier, they shouted through the barbed wire fence that prison authorities had not told them about the press conference. The Administration spokesperson

59

later blamed this on a "breakdown in communications," but would not elaborate (*Vancouver Sun*, June 6, 1981).

The press was finally permitted to hear the prisoners' side of the story. The riot was sparked by ill-feeling that had been building up for some time. Initially, it had begun as a protest by a few prisoners over what they considered to be preferential treatment by staff in the rationing of food. The recent changes in the pay structure, too, were cited: the daily rate increased, but the actual amount they received was less; no pay if they were prevented from working by the supervisor's absence; income for personal necessities was tied to jobs, but these were too scarce to go around; no sick benefits for the chronically ill beyond five days; and those on educational or vocational programmes were paid less than those in 'production'. The pay of those in 'production' had been raised to $2.00, with the present rate ranging from $1.60 to a maximum of $6.45 *per day*. Over a quarter of the prisoners were in university programmes, and many more were taking other forms of training.

In addition, the prisoners had been complaining for some time about the uncertainty of parole eligibility. "The parole system is non-existent," one prisoner said. "We're doing more time than ever before, nobody's getting out of here...." The Mandatory Supervision set-up was another important issue — the prisoners complained that the same 'non-reasons' used to put them in 'the hole' applied to Mandatory Supervision as well.

The Acting Warden had admitted to the *Ottawa Citizen* (June 4, 1981) that no ultimatum had been issued by the prisoners during the riot — just his own implied threat of using the R.C.M.P., police, and army troops, all heavily armed. "Because there were no hostages [taken]," he revealed, "the inmates really had no bargaining power or strength to force us into any sort of treaty." According to one prisoner, "There was never any thought to taking hostages even though the opportunity was there."

Damages from the riot were estimated to be anywhere from two to twelve million dollars. One report had it that over 40% of the prison was totally destroyed, while another said that "damage to the hospital and administration buildings is very superficial... to the kitchen and dining areas is moderate, and while damage to the living area is the heaviest, it is doubtful if it is extremely serious" (*Globe & Mail*, June 6, 1981).

An agreement was reached after negotiations between a four-member Inmate Committee and prison management. The presence of an R.C.M.P. squad plus guard dogs helped create the necessary atmosphere for the Warden to impress on the prisoners that if they would not move to a new tent city peacefully, force would be used.

Furthermore, disciplinary action was to be taken if the ring-leaders could be found. An internal inquiry would then be conducted where prisoners were assured that, in the words of the Warden, "Nobody's under interrogation... this isn't the Gestapo..." (*Globe & Mail*, June 8, 1981).

Nine days following the riot, the prisoners were housed in a tent city lacking even basic living necessities. There were no plans for a wholesale transfer "just because their living quarters were damaged." But plans were being made for the prisoners to rebuild the damaged prison, even though, as one contractor put it, "The supervision problem... would be impossible for any private contractor, the unions would not allow it, and the inmates are just not skilled" (*Vancouver Sun*, June 8, 1981).

Ten prisoners, thought to have been instrumental in initiating the June riot, were transferred to Eastern penitentiaries.

While living in the tent city, the prisoners were deprived of recreational and educational programmes, visits, normal hygiene conditions, and many other features normally sanctioned in federal penitentiaries. Tension and distrust was at an all-time high between prisoners and guards, as well as among prisoners themselves. Guards did not like to enter the tents during the day, and refused to at night. It was apparent that for the most part, little order was kept.

An editorial in *The Province* in June of 1981 included the following:

> Clearly the upgrading of institutions and the building of new, modern prisons with the benefit of new insights into practical design, have made little difference in the outlook of prison life.

There seem to be more, rather than fewer, uprisings across Canada.

# Kent

> In prison more than elsewhere one cannot afford to be casual. One cannot endure a penalty so monstrous as the lack of freedom without demanding of one's mind and body a labour at once delicate and brutal. (George Jackson — Soledad Brothers)

Kent Maximum Security Institution is situated about forty miles from Vancouver near Agassiz in the Fraser Valley. Opened in August 1979 with a capacity for 192 prisoners in a modern university campus setting, it was hailed as "...an exemplary model in providing progressive programmes for offenders in a humane and secure environment." And, Kent provides "opportunities to upgrade work skills or learn new ones" which will "help [prisoners] assume personal responsibility while preparing for release back into society." Apparently, too, the security system, which was so sophisticated that it must be kept a secret, "...was one of the most advanced in the world."

Two months after Kent opened, a fire and riot resulted in $30,000 worth of damage. Prisoners took a guard hostage and demanded an end to unnecessary body searches, denial of visiting privileges and the use of solitary confinement for minor infractions. A month-long strike-riot took place to protest, in part, the postponement of the 'rehabilitative' part of the Kent programme, which the guards complained would be dangerous because it would permit prisoners to mingle too much. They also vetoed the common dining room (which meant that prisoners would have to eat alone in their cells) and subjected many to skin frisks for no apparent reason. In order to avert an impending catastrophe, the prisoners agreed to end the strike.

All of which was dismissed by the Warden as "...part of the ironing out of wrinkles in a new institution." It is interesting to note that many of the guards had previously worked at the recently closed B.C. Pen, and that they were in the process, once again, of negotiating a new contract.

The usual senseless transfer to Eastern penitentiaries of ten so-called 'troublemakers' did little to lessen the mounting tension. Both staff and prisoners continued to warn of conflicts which could only lead to trouble. For example, in March 1980 the prisoners had boycotted the gym in a one-day protest, and the overcrowded P.C.U. held a hunger strike in another incident. As well, four guards in the solitary confinement H Unit had been charged in provincial court with assault. According to an unimpressed Warden, the complaints were "just problems resulting from the newness of the institution."

Incidents of 'slashings' and 'sprees' continued on a regular basis. Toward the end of 1980, a letter sent to the Commissioner from the Prisoners' Committee included:

> Conditions here are resulting in a strong and rapidly growing amount of tension which could very easily turn into a very explosive situation if not curbed. A few months ago, a member of the prison population was stabbed to death. We were locked up for the rest of that evening. Now, when a few windows get broken and an office gets burnt (no injuries) we all get locked up, with visits, phone calls and correspondence suspended and a limit of two meals a day. That places the value of human life at only a fraction of the value placed on windows. The only way we feel the tension will even begin to reduce is if for once, serious and sincere communication between the Administration and the prison population via the elected Prisoners' Committee begins and remains.

Another letter, received in late January 1981, describes the kind of treatment prisoners were repeatedly subjected to. It reads, in part:

> Yesterday, good old Hollinger [one of the sharp-shooters in the B.C. Pen tactical squad which had killed Mary Steinhauser during the 1975 B.C. Pen hostage-taking] went into the cells to spray radioactive something or other... gave one of our guys a shove and took a swing

at him. Our boy defended himself which resulted in Hollinger getting beat up. Then came immediate mass confusion — entire joint to lock-up. Everyone wondering if it was a hostage-taking.

Suddenly 30 to 50 staff came into the courtyard in full riot gear. From above the school area, guards smashed out windows with the butts of their AK 15's to take aim at the prisoners. We went, and got locked up... later treated to a systematic skin frisk... locked up for two more days.

Never in my life have I seen such an over-reaction... could easily have erupted into a mass blood bath. Why such an overreaction to a nothing incident?

Meanwhile, in H Unit (solitary confinement) systematic harassment continued. Fifty-four pages expressing strong concern about the safety of their brothers in this Unit were delivered in February 1981 via the 'back door' to known sympathetic outsiders. All but a few refused to sign their letters for the very real fear of reprisals, such as being transferred to Eastern Canada. A few excerpts are recorded here:

As active members of the Kent Lifers Organisation, we hereby collectively protest the use and the management of the infamous H Unit. [It is] in conflict with the Commissioner's Directives and therefore deserves to be sealed forever.

Many horror tales have been told about this Unit. Most of them are loathing in nature and border on madness. The bulk of our information is undocumented in the traditional sense, however we have listened carefully, and we do believe that the information is factual.

We find it extremely ironic that Canadians can condemn others in other countries for inflicting pain and damage to their people when these same practices exist within this country in full view of the government.

We would ask that this Unit be thoroughly investigated immediately before any further damage is done to those who are presently encaged there, and that the findings be made public.

The Administration is locking up newcomers in solitary also, with the explanation that there are no empty cells in the population. Meanwhile, there is a full unit that can house 24 prisoners that is not in operation. The Prisoners' Committee is not allowed to see these men, but can only go through correspondence which is censored. If a prisoner in solitary is having trouble with the custody, obviously they're not going to let him write about it to the Committee.

Nothing has been done concerning our defense regarding the segregation review hearings. They ask the very guards who inflict beatings, provocations, physical and verbal abuse... they do not call the con out to hear his defense.

...placing prisoners in a cell, hand-cuffed and shackled for days at a time and taking away all clothes, bedding, personal effects and food... unnecessary use of mace, fire-hosing and pointing guns at cons... unnecessary beatings upon hand-cuffed prisoners... 10 minutes for showers every five days... only 20 minutes exercise every 2 days... locked up sometimes for 24 hours a day for weeks at a time....

... prisoners have been in there for periods up to and over 6 months. It's shocking to see such a pretty-looking new prison like Kent carry on the bad practices that made the B.C. Pen the cesspool it was.

The keepers of these tombs in the name of government, peace and security have had their own characters so debased that they themselves have lost their humanity... have become the club of tyrants.

It's not completely fair to say that the Kent Admin-istration has not implemented some changes. Tables and beds have been installed in the cells, prisoners no longer have to sleep on the floor.... can write to the Prisoners' Committee although not all this correspondence gets through. If there is a rumour that a prisoner has been beaten up by staff, it has started to happen that the Administration will produce the prisoner for inspection by the Prisoners' Committee.... It has taken over a year and a half to get this far.

Prisoners have struck, rioted, burned and taken hos-tages, always at a great cost to themselves, all to bring public attention to their situation. Again this is yet another plea — for a complete enquiry into the unfair methods with which prison justice is dispensed, and a tormented cry for help in abolishing some of those practices which are not only cruel, but irreversibly mind-destroying as well.

We have been sentenced to prison *as* the punishment, not *to be punished*.

After reading the lengthy list of people to whom the prisoners requested that copies be sent — politicians, prison officials, church groups, human rights and civil liberties organisations, media, friendly lawyers and prisoner supporters — a plan was devised whereby local members from the lawyer and activist groups would send a covering letter along with the fifty-four pages to the others on the list, with the exception of the media. The letter would emphasise the urgency and the fact that we had before us the 'investigation' *before* instead of *after* the riot, which appeared inevitable. If no response resulted, we would then send it to the media with another covering letter describing our efforts to forestall imminent disturbances. If all the parties still failed to respond, we would have had documented evidence to show how every human effort had been made to negotiate while there was still time.

Whether this plan would have succeeded is never to be known, because, unfortunately, it was dropped.

Not even a letter, dated May 21, 1981, from M.P. Svend Robinson, the N.D.P. critic of the Solicitor-General's department, was able to elicit any reasonable reaction from Kent's Warden:

> ...very concerned about serious allegations of beatings. I am getting frankly rather angry at your apparent failure to recognise the potential for serious problems at Kent. The Prisoners' Committee has submitted a very reasonable proposal asking for... access to H Unit on a regular basis. Millhaven and Archambault provide such access. Other concerns are... why are craft programmes virtually non-existent?... the failure of your office to reply to proposals from the Prisoners' Committee — some *thirty* within the last four months. (Emphasis added)
>
> Finally, the rule of law does *not* stop at the entrance to Kent. What constitutes an assault outside Kent also constitutes an assault inside Kent. The way that prisoners are treated today will be reflected in how they act tomorrow!

Disregarding all these distress signals, the Solicitor-General responded on June 8th as follows: "...so far as there being a crisis in the prisons... the fact that no demands were made by inmates during any of the incidents... is some evidence that they were not motivated by a lack of reform...."

Not unexpectedly, within six months, Kent 'came down'. Over 100 prisoners were involved in a burning and smashing spree resulting in an estimated $100,000 damage. No hostages were taken. Although prisoners had the opportunity to smash guards' control panels, they did not — in fact, they even forewarned certain staff members. Five prisoners were injured. And in spite of the months of plodding efforts by the Prisoners' Committee and other concerned parties to head off the disaster, the authorities were quoted as being 'still puzzled' over what sparked the rampage.

By coincidence, the more than 4,400 federal prison guards who had been negotiating a new contract had their contract demands settled *within a week* after the riot. Also, newspapers reported that thousands of dollars worth of riot combat equipment had been purchased and was on hand awaiting use in each prison.

A total of thirty-eight charges, including arson, public mischief and attempted murder, were laid against seven prisoners as a result of the June riot at Kent. Most of the charges were dropped, leaving three of the accused with one- to three-year consecutive sentences to serve. But these weren't the only repercussions.

In a letter dated November 15, 1981, one of the prisoners who was being returned from the speedy post-riot transfer of the Prisoners' Committee describes this misfortune which befell him en route:

> Something I found strange, was as if they wanted us doped up. When we asked for medication the nurse gave us a needle without bitching. I got over 6 shots and was like a vegetable, a zombie, really stoned by the time we landed. Called to the C.S.C. officer in charge and the nurse, expressed my fears about getting beat because it was too weird — the vibes were too hateful, and two Living Unit officers who I had conflict with when in Kent

population were there. Then I asked for another shot before landing, to dull the pain I knew would come. The nurse gave it to me like she knew.

Now myself being the last to unload and the perfect setup.... They got the mace out and the billy clubs... rains of hits from front and back. I thought they would never stop. I blacked out but only for a few seconds. Came half to. Blood all over my face and head, everything spinning, guards standing around laughing. Then I felt my leg shaken, looked, and there's a dog-handler putting his dog on me. He let it chew on me and rip my clothes, took it off, then put it on me again. I couldn't move. This dog was shaking and dragging me, then I passed out. Came to in Vancouver. Or half to.

Couldn't eat for 17 days... can't even remember seeing you in court, or even being there. I've seen outside doctors. They say there's something wrong with me. Having sort of blackouts sometimes... always tired, dizzy, bad head-aches, something weird with my speech. Can't concentrate... this letter's taken 2½ hours.

It was an attempted murder on me. Read that log I wrote during the riot. It was only a matter of time. Now everyone is wondering who is next. I want to lay charges, but hear nothing. Maybe you can check it out. Also six prisoners in an open window van seen the whole thing. I don't want to lay it down. Where's it to end? Who's next?

In order to draw media attention to this man's precarious state of health, and as a show of support, I spent the day of November 9, 1981, in the Kent parking lot, standing at the wire fence facing H Unit, a distance of approximately 250 feet. For refusing to leave when requested, a summons was served two months later with the usual 'trespassing on penitentiary property' charge, punishable on summary conviction to six months imprisonment, a $500 fine, or both. When the 'offence' eventually came to court, it was dismissed on the basis that it was "...at best, a borderline case."

Unfortunately, the crucial issue — the setting of a dog on a semi-conscious prisoner at Abbotsford airport late one night — was overlooked. Nor was there any response from Amnesty

International to the request to investigate this case under their mandate dealing with ill-treatment and torture.

Overcrowding, double-bunking, cutbacks in education and recreation programmes, accompanied by confrontations, continue to persist. The C.S.C.'s solution — expanding Kent by more than 50% (about 100 cells) — can hardly be expected to provide the 'greater security' or 'smoother operation' that prison officials claim to want. That a larger prison does *not* ensure better security becomes obvious when we read of the two prisoners who walked out the front gate of Kent, in spite of its 'magnificent, sophisticated security system' (*The Advance*, May 5, 1982).

Nor does prison size change attitudes. In one case, two prisoners in solitary confinement had appealed to the Classification Board to be returned to the general population. Despite the Classification Board's recommendation that they be returned, the Warden refused. It took a B.C. Court Order, which referred to the "devastation of prolonged solitary confinement in isolation," to get the two out of solitary confinement (*Vancouver Sun*, April 1, 1982).

Neither at Kent Maximum Security nor at any other prison across Canada are fundamental changes in the attitudes of those involved in the Canadian Prison System realistic, caught up as they all are in the web of the prison scene.

Little has changed in this '...exemplary model in providing progressive programmes for offenders in a humane and secure environment' (as announced at Kent's gala opening in August 1979).

## Archambault

> No one shall be subjected to torture, or to cruel, inhuman or degrading treatment or punishment. (Article V, Universal Declaration of Human Rights)

In terms of ferocity, the name of Archambault in Canadian prison circles now matches that of Attica in the United States. Opened in 1969, Archambault is a Maximum Security prison constructed for 429 occupants, about thirty miles north of Montréal.

In 1976, a four-month non-violent work stoppage succeeded in providing the prisoners with slightly better living conditions. They had expressed frustrations about the lack of physical contact with their visitors — one prisoner described not having been able to embrace his wife or children for fifteen years. The Manifesto which they presented included among its sixteen demands that their right to a normal and healthy sex life be recognised; an end to the restrictive visiting and correspondence conditions; immediate formation of a Citizens' Committee with decision-making powers over the Administration and prison life; a Prisoners' Committee whose constitution be accepted in its present form; abolition and immediate closure of the segregation wing; immediate improvements in health care, listing six specific areas; and others covering recreation, work, parole, food, etc.

This 110-day strike appears to have been the high point in an otherwise turbulent thirteen-year period. During that time, there were five hostage-takings, two prison officials murdered (outside the prison area), and sixteen prisoners killed — six in 1979 alone.

On the night of July 25, 1982, Archambault was the scene of an escape attempt by two prisoners who were serving minimum 25-year sentences. The attempt escalated into a major incident which resulted in three guards being brutally slain and the two instigators found dead, having taken cyanide capsules in what was later recognised as a suicide pact.

Tracing through the maze of subsequent reports (both national and international), press releases, articles, interviews and analyses which this 'worst prison riot in Canadian history' produced, one would expect that this information would have contributed to the culmination of all that was known, and not yet known, about the faults and weaknesses already documented by the 1977 MacGuigan Report, and that this accumulated knowledge would lay the basis for a more stable prison system. Only sound political analyses of the role of prisons in a capitalist society can satisfactorily explain why this was not to be.

To offset the urgent need for a full, public and impartial inquiry into the entire Archambault riot, the Inspector-General, A. Wrenshall, was ordered by the Solicitor-General on July 26, 1982, to look into the incident. The Inspector-General interviewed every component — staff, the union of the Solicitor-General's employees, Québec Police Force and Crown Prosecutor — all except the prisoners, whom he felt "...would best be handled if conducted by the Institution's Preventive Security Officer." A Police Inquiry and a Coroner's Inquiry were also taking place at this time.

Notable among the list of forty-six findings by the Board are the following:

> The use of [tear] gas was effective for its intended purpose and was justified; the response by the institutional health care staff in examining all inmates at the first reasonable opportunity was adequate; the Crisis Management operation was adequate and effective; and, there is a need to expeditiously complete a study to determine the most secure and humane method of incarcerating inmates who have been sentenced to a minimum of 25 years. A review of the files of the two prisoners who instigated the action indicated that both had appealed their 25-year sentences. In the case of [Yvon] Martin, he was veritably obsessed with his appeal.... since these sentences have been around for only six years, the Service's knowledge is still fairly limited.

The sixteen recommendations dealt entirely with improvement of existing measures for protection of staff and security members with two exceptions, which related to the need for a study dealing with the special problems posed by 25-year minimum sentences and the need for the "Service to be notified by the courts as early as possible of the decision relating to an inmate's appeal case."

In a later analysis of the Wrenshall Report, Steve Fineberg of the Montréal-based Prisoners' Rights Committee (l'Office des Droits des Détenu-e-s — l'O.D.D.) has written that this report was

> classified confidential, and submitted only to Bob Kaplan and the Correctional Service, but its partial publication has since been achieved through the *Access to Information Act.* According to the information thus obtained, on July

26, the Board was briefed at Québec Regional Head-
quarters... 'The Board concluded its on-site inquiry on
August 4, 1982, with a debriefing of the Deputy Commissioner... as well as the Institutional Warden.'

To be more specific, the Inspector-General acquainted the
Solicitor-General's office with "the extent... and strength of
the anti-prisoner sentiment [which] caused the guards 'to want
to react violently against the inmates'." It also detailed "the
probable duration of violent anti-prisoner reaction" which found
its way into the Report's official Finding No. 43: "There is a
need for the Service to become more actively involved in assisting
staff to better control and release their emotions both as a
contingency in the event of prison disturbances and following
such experiences."

Fineberg further queries "why in the light of this abundant
warning, sufficient precautions were not taken to prevent the
free rein of exactly this kind of violent hostility toward prisoners?...." and "What part of the abusive treatment detailed
in the various reports occurred after August 4th when the
Solicitor-General's office was definitively put on notice by the
Inspector-General regarding violent behaviour by the guards?"

The answer is found in the fact that detailed accounts contained in the Kolb Report, the Maleville Report, the United
Church Report and the Amnesty International Report all
demonstrated that mistreatment of prisoners did occur *after*
August 4th, the date of the Inspector-General's Report to the
Solicitor-General. There can be no question that the government
was not alerted to the possibility of the subsequent actions by
the guards. It was forewarned, yet it took no steps to avoid
the predictable consequences. This was further confirmed when
Svend Robinson, M.P., presented evidence in the House of
Commons on August 26th, based on five hours meeting with
prisoners and staff.

At a later date, January 20, 1983, lawyer Renée Millette
included a precise timetable in the Motion filed with the Québec
Superior Court on behalf of seventeen prisoners who wished
to institute private prosecutions against their tormentors.

Fineberg unerringly concludes with considerable impact that
"Given the government's knowledge before the above events

occurred, its refusal or inability to prevent these events from taking place, and the shocking consequences of its inactivity, the need for a full, independent and impartial public inquiry... becomes clear and urgent. Until the damning suggestions of responsibility have been investigated and rebutted, these persons... lack the moral authority to occupy their offices."

What follows is a brief outline of the various national and international investigations which, culminating in the report by the reputable Amnesty International, finally forced the Canadian Government to proceed with their version of an independent inquiry. Interestingly enough, nowhere does one find the note of warning sounded in Fineberg's analysis of the Wrenshall Report — that the Canadian Government be held culpable for the ensuing torture of prisoners. Because only the main points in these reports are mentioned here, it should not necessarily be concluded that the investigators were remiss except where it is specifically suggested.

*A Report to the International Human Rights Law Group*, Washington, D.C. (September 23, 1982), by Attorney Charles E.M. Kolb, includes the following:

> Given the repeated accusations surfacing in the press and from the civil-rights attorneys of brutality (by the guards) towards, and even torture of, certain inmates, the Director acknowledged that some inmates had been 'harassed' by a 'minority' of the guards.... He had told those guards that such behaviour (like keeping prisoners awake all night by banging on their cell doors) was not conducive to a return to more normal conditions.... This was the only form of harassment acknowledged by the Director.
>
> The detention cells, or the 'hole', warrants special concern.... Sixteen cells are reserved for the most troublesome.... Fourteen of these contain nothing more than a wooden pallet, mattress and metal toilet. Ceilings are extremely high and the fluorescent light unreachable.... Food is served through metal openings in the doors that are fastened shut from the outside. Two of these cells contain no pallet and no toilet... flushing mechanisms are located outside the cells and can only be activated by a Correctional Officer.

On July 28 [three days after the five deaths took place] some forty journalists were allowed into Archambault. Tear gas had been used on the inmates... and [Warden] LeMarier expressed some concern about the lingering effects throughout the institution. Nevertheless, journalists were allowed in and lawyers were not. The gravity of the Archambault riot and the potential for serious charges brought against inmates suspected of involvement clearly warrant the presence of counsel. There is in my view no legitimate basis for having denied access to attorneys (for ten days) while having allowed — in fact expressly invited — journalists... inmates hung placards out the windows [as the journalists entered] stating THEY HAVE GASSED US.

Tear gas was also sprayed directly into some of the sandwiches and into the milk which the inmates were supposed to eat.... One inmate had reportedly been held by two guards while tear gas was shot directly into his mouth at point blank range.... at least one reported instance of a guard urinating on sandwiches, making the inmate eat them, and then forcing him to say how good they were.

On July 27... inmate placed on the floor face down, handcuffed from behind and then beaten en route to an interrogation room where he was shoved head first into the room, smashing his head into a closed door.... interrogated but refused to confess any involvement in the riot.... asked to kneel in front of the door to his cell, and was then kicked into his cell...

...water turned off, all of his clothing, linens and mattress were removed... was left totally naked in what he said was a very cold cell...

...described seeing at one point eight guards lined up to have their boots polished by a naked inmate kneeling on the floor.

...confined in the 'hole' for several days without any food or water except what they could drink from their toilet bowls.

Some of the attorneys involved told me that one inmate who is unable to read was forced to sign a confession... guards tried to trip him and shoved him in the back with their leaded sticks after he had spoken with one of his attorneys... campaign of harassment against the attorneys and their clients.

The right to counsel guaranteed by the 1982 Constitution and the Canadian Declaration of Rights has clearly been violated since July 26, 1982, and continues to be violated (as at August 6, 1982) since no inmate may communicate with his attorney, neither by letter, telephone or even their families or by an intermediary such as the person inside the Pen generally charged with allowing outside phone calls.

My interpretation of the P.S.R. (Penitentiary Service Regulations) Article 38 would require that punishment... for the offences described in P.S.R. Article 39 cannot be predicated upon a mere suspicion of involvement in a crime or offence. It is at least arguable, and in my view extremely plausible, that punishment based upon a mere suspicion contravenes Article 9 of the Constitution Act of Canada: 'Everyone has the right not to be arbitrarily detained or imprisoned.'... that prisoners forfeit their constitutional rights when they enter prison would be absurd.

Additionally it should be stressed that *all* the inmates have suffered because of July 25 whether they participated in the violence or not. It would be a serious mistake if those Correctional officers who subjected inmates to 'cruel and unusual treatment or punishment' were permitted to escape censure.

Did the conditions inside Archambault Penitentiary violate Canada's obligations under international law as set forth in three Human Rights instruments — the Universal Declaration of Human Rights 1948, the International Covenant on Civil and Political Rights 1976, and the Standard Minimum Rules for the Treatment of Prisoners 1955? — the answer must be, yes.

**Recommendations:**

● *In addition to the investigations now underway concerning inmate misconduct, a separate, outside and objective investigation concerning Correctional officer misconduct should be made and the results released to the public. Appropriate sanctions should be invoked regarding those guards whose behaviour warrants such discipline.*

- *Regulations should be amended to provide for a broader inmate access to counsel at all pertinent times as required by Canada's Constitution.*

- *Canada's Solicitor-General should report to the Human Rights Committee... about Archambault 1982... [and] outline what steps are being taken to guarantee Canada's future compliance with the International Covenant on Civil and Political Rights. The Human Rights Committee, on its part, should monitor Canada's future compliance with the International Covenant.*

- *Canada's frank recognition that wrongs have been committed at Archambault, if accompanied by its sincere attempt to prevent them from recurring, will be the necessary first step towards a greater recognition by Canadians at home and abroad of the basic rights and freedoms of all persons.*

While Mr. Kolb's impassioned conclusion is a laudable one, he obviously had not absorbed the full impact of the P.S.R.'s masterful ambiguity regarding dissociation. Penitentiary Service Regulation 40(1)(a) authorises the Warden to consign prisoners to segregation "where the institutional head is satisfied that [it is] (a) for the maintenance of good order and discipline in the institution, or (b) in the best interests of the inmate." Translated into the constant threat hanging over every prisoner, this Section comes into full play if the Warden personally considers there is reason — for suspicion of... (or) conspiracy to... with no avenue for appeal by the prisoner whatsoever.

There are religious groups which have over the years demonstrated their deep concern about the fate of prisoners and their families. The same spirit which moves church people in Latin America to acts of great courage as they identify with the poor and the repressed is finally manifesting itself in our country. I have the good fortune of receiving much encouragement from this community in the common cause of changing public attitudes and bureaucratic strangleholds.

Bishop Remi J. DeRoo, addressing a group of criminal lawyers and judges in April 1984 in Victoria, B.C., made his views known: "The Canadian criminal justice system is vindictive and favours the rich over the poor.... Incarceration is a total failure, it's seen as a very vindictive system, and we know the vast majority of people in prisons are non-violent.... We have two systems of law, a system for the rich and powerful and a system of law for the poor and the marginalised groups. Capital punishment and humiliating alternatives to incarceration are morally deplorable because they do not recognise the value and dignity of human life."

More recently, Reverend Morton Paterson of the United Church of Canada won a $100,000 two-year scholarship to study the Canadian criminal justice system from a theological standpoint. His stated intention to share mutual concerns and 'angers' around imprisonment bodes well for his research and, by extension, for prisoners.

Reverend Wayne A. Smith added the full weight of the Presbyterian Church in Canada to the many demands for an independent public inquiry into the Archambault Riot. In a letter to the *Globe & Mail* on November 5, 1982, as Moderator of the 108th General Assembly, he declared that this issue "affects every Canadian [for] we are the society that placed men in this institution.... We need to know what went wrong and what needs to be changed.... The peace and security of us all is at stake here." Reverend Smith's church has already publicly called for "...parole eligibility to be reduced to ten years for first-degree murder and seven years for second-degree" — a bold stance to take considering the current vengeful atmosphere.

In accordance with a directive from the 29th General Council of the United Church, Moderator Clarke MacDonald met with Chaplains of the Federal Penitentiary Service and those at Archambault prison in order to determine the current situation of prisoners there. Visits were arranged for the 9th and 30th of September, 1982, from which he reported (in part) that:

> Between seventy-five and 150 inmates were sent for varying lengths of time into segregation (the hole) and approximately fifty were finally identified as having actively taken part in the riot.
>
> The rest of the inmates were accused of participating passively and were therefore 'socially responsible' and penalised as a consequence. The Director of Security indicated that this was a 'social price' which they had to pay.

*Treatment of the Inmates:*

It is alleged that tear gas was used extensively and repeatedly for a week or two... served cold meals of two sandwiches each twice a day.... This regime was maintained until late September, although the number of sandwiches was increased and hot soup, hot water for tea or coffee and occasionally a small container of beans was added.... One cold rainy day, inmates were harassed by gun fire to keep them moving while in the yard....

There have been a variety of reports of what could only be called cruel and unusual or degrading treatment... especially the Kolb report. While not in a position to judge the reliability of this report, he [the Moderator] is somewhat appalled by the facile manner in which it has been dismissed by the Solicitor-General of Canada.

*Meeting with the Inmate Committee:*

They disassociated themselves from the tragic events without blaming the instigators... [urged] pressure on the legislators to change the 25-year mandatory part of the life sentence [which] leaves a person totally helpless. Made the following observation of how the system works: "Some inmates find wisdom to cope with society again only after lengthy incarceration, others become aware very quickly; but the system treats them all the same. It is as if I break my arm, I go to a doctor who puts my arm in a cast for a period of time. According to the book, my arm will be cured only after three casts. However, when I return, my arm is completely cured. Nevertheless, because the book says it has to have three casts, the doctor insists on putting on the second and third cast. This is an example of the stupidity of the system."

In the words of another one of them: "We could have gone into the gory details, but to do that would jeopardise our future and we have to live here."

*Visitation to 'The Hole':*

All young men, and most had been there for over a month. One described the first fifteen days as 'hell' — nothing to read, no radio or anything to listen to, nothing to write with. All he could do for twenty-four hours a day was stare at the ceiling and walls.

*Meeting with the Assistant Director of Security:*

Expressed his fear of the consequences of the projection that with the 25-year mandatory aspect of life sentences, in the year 2000 there will be 400 25-year mandatory lifers in Québec [alone] — almost the present population of Archambault.

Questioned in regard to the 'hole': "I was never," he affirmed, "ashamed of what went on in the hole until the period between June 25 and several weeks ago.... I cannot, however, verify any of the hypotheses. If I approach an area, guards 'warn' other guards of my whereabouts." While he understood this desire for revenge, he rejected it as any kind of practical solution.

*Meeting with the Guards:*

Asked what they would suggest... to expedite reha-bilitation, one answered: "Those who are closest to being released should have the most privileges and work an eight-hour day as in society, for the same salary as for someone from outside... have a bank account and be trained so that when they leave prison they can become adults very quickly."

They complained about only "very, very rarely" being consulted about "penitentiary reform measures... only heard about conjugal visits by radio and TV. Now they are talking about double-bunking... a non-solution which would over-populate the prison and bring more problems and more violence...."

*Conclusions:*

...that justice may be seen to be done in our society, that the dehumanising aspects of our prison system which have been noted in many reports, including this one, may be ameliorated....

## Recommendations:

- *That a full and independent inquiry be called by the Solicitor-General.*

- *That since guards, administrators and prisoners agree that life sentences with 25-year mandatory before parole eligibility are creating a pressure-cooker effect... urge the Solicitor-General to study the present and long-term effects of this at once, with a view to recommending creative alternatives.*

● *That congregations and parishes in areas where there are prisons of any kind take a greater interest in what is taking place... and be supportive of community-based programmes for ex-inmates to assist them to return to society as creative individuals...*

From Rev. MacDonald's Appendix: "It was reported that eventually the postings of the guards seeking revenge through violence were changed in an attempt by the Administration to stop the harassment." At a later date, when informally discussing the Archambault case with several guards in other Québec prisons who themselves had been moved to other locations following similar situations, I found that the common denominator was their wonder why guards who were personally involved in any way during a hostage-taking were not *immediately* transferred out of the highly charged atmosphere.

To his great credit, Rev. MacDonald did not settle for merely submitting a report calling for an inquiry, but persisted in his demands. While he accepted the Solicitor-General's offer to interview five prisoners who 'allegedly were abused at Archambault,' it was not as a compromise, for he had also arranged with the United Church to retain this particular mandate even after his two-year term as Moderator expired. His subsequent January 1983 report indicated:

> that the allegations of harassment and intimidation, of torture by hitting, gassing and threatening; of humiliation, of obscene acts... have been largely substantiated by the first-hand information provided by these prisoners... some are prepared and able to identify guards....
>
> In the light of the above... strongly reaffirm the need for a full, independent public inquiry... as soon as possible... supported by many responsible voices, including the Kolb and Maleville reports.

At this point I shall succumb to the temptation to quote extensively from Rev. MacDonald's painful interviews with these five prisoners, not so much to sharpen the reader's sensibilities, as to authenticate the true nature of the Canadian prison system. If shock therapy is needed to persuade Canadians that they dare not tolerate centres of torture within their own communities, one cogent argument stands out: as well as the victim who may die or linger in agony, the brutaliser is also brutalised. Prison guards and police, who use their position to batter and kill those in their custody, are joining the ranks of the violence-prone members of our society. Do the 'crimes' of the 'criminals' warrant the uncontrolled sadism of their keepers? In such a climate, people can go 'missing', as the police take on the role of high judge executioner.

Having said that, note must also be taken of the toll exacted in the human condition generated by this most alienating environment of all. It is seldom recognised that those with unlimited authority over others are also sacrificed. Nowhere are the adversarial lines more alarmingly drawn than between the keeper and the kept. In the words of Dr. Bruno M. Cormier: "...few individuals in a democratic society are exposed day after day, year after year, to so much paranoid thinking as are prison guards — the only profession where the basic challenge is to resist the ever present temptation to become persecutors" (*The Watchers and The Watched*, 1975).

And in her own sensitive analysis in *The Politics of Punishment*, journalist Lorraine Begley concludes: "Little wonder, then, that those employed in prisons also find the experience dehumanising. Guards have the impossible task of attempting to function like normal, decent persons in a situation where they are universally hated. Walking every day into a wall of unremitting bitterness, working in a world constantly at war, guards pay for their jobs with shortened life expectancies, a high rate of alcoholism and drug abuse, and an increased incidence of marital and family problems" (*New Maritimes*, November 1984).

The torment is a shared experience, whether all the actors realise it or not.

Following is a resumé of Rev. MacDonald's interviews:

*Prisoner No. 1*:
    In three weeks I did not get six hours sleep... received two meals in three weeks... only meals I received were the days that the lawyers were there to see us... held down and handcuffed and pissed upon... through the night they would beat me and at the time of one severe beating I was hit in the solar plexus with a billy bat...

caused me to puke on one of the guards and they beat me for doing this... after exhaustion and lack of food I began to hallucinate and things were not always clear... made to get into the shower on my hands and knees. Spic & Span and Lysol detergent was put on my hair and upper body... water for only thirty seconds then turned off... for two weeks no way of washing... smelled terrible... one day I was gassed six times... a stream of it in my face and up my nose... had a hole in my intestines, called a 'traumatic hernia' from billy bat which they stuck into my abdomen... put a Bible on my head and pounded... it leaves no marks... when you've got 25 years you say 'what's the use of getting up today, what's the use of taking food off the tray'... I thought they were going to kill me on a number of occasions... when I was in the hospital I would plead for the nurse to give me a painkiller and they would not call her... would pop a shotgun in my face....

*Prisoner No. 2:*

I asked for a lawyer on the third day but never saw one... for nine days they beat me, but not seriously... more intimidation than physical abuse, although there was some of that... they would slam the food through the slot so that it would fall on the floor... not fit to eat but better than starving... guards took their name tags off and all their insignia... no lawyers, no police, just guards... gassed through the slot in the door... three or four times a day... your eyes get very sore... had no clothes, no bedding, no mattress, no water, no toilet paper... fortunately because of lack of food I had very few bowel movements... taken to see the police handcuffed and shackled and had to run a gauntlet to get there... when I was given pyamas they were dipped into water before passed on to me, and the guards or someone urinated on the mattress... other guys were really tortured more than me... I could hear them shouting and crying... they had a mock hanging for one guy. I saw the rope which they swung in front of my door as they went by... I could hear the guy next door choking....

*Prisoner No. 3:*

I saw one man beaten with heavy balls that were contained in a kind of pouch on a long string... they would come into the cells at night and beat on me with long clubs... from time to time on the heels, ribs, with batons... made to bend over and they would put cigarettes up to my eyes, not *in* my eyes, but the heat would burn my eyelids... gassed two or three times a day... they took a sheet and made a kind of rope and hung me by the head on my tiptoes and then after the air was cut off so that I was just about suffocating, they let me go... we heard a lot of things happening which we did not see... the shouts and cries of men being beaten... they brought a linoleum knife in and said they were going to cut us up in little pieces... I reacted with fear... they put the knife against my testicles... I was naked for three weeks... the end of a club was pushed into my rectum... gassed and beaten regularly for ten to fifteen days....

*Prisoner No. 4:*

When prisoners pounded on the doors because they were not getting food and could not wash the mace from their faces, they were told to stop or they would be gassed again. They did stop but were gassed just the same... you were afraid to eat the sandwiches in case they had been polluted... made to kneel in the corner and was hit, not enough to bruise but enough to tease and to hurt... totally naked in the cell with no mattress or blanket... toilet was filthy... they would pull my hair out and pull the hair in my beard... warn me 'if you mention any of this to your lawyer we'll make it worse for you'... was often hit with a club and they stepped on my bare toes with their heavy boots....

*Prisoner No. 5:*

They took small cans of gas and held me down while forcing me to open my mouth, then they would shoot the mace into my mouth... one guy was taken into the shower and they turned very hot water on him. I could hear him screaming... the man in the next cell was made to walk with his hands shackled around his legs... three men held me down when I was sleeping and one of them pissed on me... I have the name of the man who did this. One man [name given] they put his face to his excrement. They did that to other inmates as well... they told me that one of my pals was ready to identify me as an instigator in the riot... forced someone to say it was me... when he denied it they hit him some more, this went on for twenty minutes... next day they got me. 'You're going to confess or we'll kill you.' I really got scared... in the courtyard, handcuffed and made to lay on my back in a kind of trough or drain... tore a towel in two and put it over my face very tight and then with a kettle of cold water they dripped it into my mouth... nose covered and I couldn't breathe through it... felt I was going to drown... gasping for breath...

They asked me questions... pulled my hair, slapped my face, I began to bleed from my nose... I was exhausted... then I made the admission they wanted me to make... I was not able to sleep for days... not just physical pain, but mental pain, confusion and hallucination... a few had more punishment than I had... police saw me twice, wanted me to make a declaration... 'You're going to talk or we'll get it out of you. We won't hit you, there are others here who will do it for us.' They then said 'since this bastard doesn't want to coöperate, take him back to his cell. Fix him up good. I want to see him again.' Then things happened in the cell. After that they took me back to see the police. I signed the declaration. I could not take any more. It implicated a lot of other men as well as myself. After I had done this, they said very sarcastically, 'It wasn't so hard, was it. If you want to coöperate when this comes to court, we could arrange no more charges... and a parole for you.'

Water torture was also a favorite method of the American forces in South Vietnam when I was working there in the late Sixties as a Hospital Administrator. Nor was it unusual for the G.I.s (some of them young Canadians) to regale us — fellow whites — with their prowess at gang-raping young Vietnamese girls. It is now acknowledged how the havoc of that particular war has yet to be tallied. It left its veterans physically damaged from the Agent Orange herbicides, and psychologically damaged from the daily massacres and tortures in which they participated.

In Oslo, Norway, in 1971 at the International Commission of Enquiry into U.S. Crimes in Indochina, again young American (and Canadian) Vietnam veterans described to us the barbaric acts which were part of their daily routine. The lesson to be drawn is that any similar violent behaviour on the part of our own self-styled law-and-order police and prison guards must be repudiated and brought to a dead stop.

The Maleville Report, presented in December 1982 by the Paris-based International Federation of Human Rights, was the next to

> demonstrate beyond any doubt that the right to counsel was withdrawn from the prisoners for a period of ten days. Nor was the complicity of the police in the serious abuse of prisoners in any doubt. As a consequence, the credibility of the administration of justice... has been badly impaired. If Canada wishes through the agency of the Solicitor-General and the Québec Ministry of Justice to re-establish social and individual justice, they must act together so that (1) the legal proceedings currently underway be suspended until (2) an impartial public inquiry has shed light on events at Archambault since July 25, 1982.

With regard to the violence of the prisoners, this report makes the unique commentary that

> no one can deny how infernal and vile that night was. Yet we would be deceiving ourselves if we were to content ourselves by qualifying it as bestial; it is, after all, true that 'man alone, despite his reason, does that which the animals without reason have never done.' We must therefore seek out the source of the violence so as to prevent it from manifesting itself again.

And once again the factor which

> conspire[d] toward the fatal events of that night [was seen to be] the existence of incompressible sentences: in the case in point, the 25-year minimum eligibility sentences to which the two prisoners who set off the tragedy were condemned. Nothing could illustrate this point more clearly

than the terms 'walking bomb' and 'time bomb' used by the persons encountered.

Another keen observation is found in Thierry Maleville's comment about the food situation described in every report:

> Of all the material needs that must be supplied to inmates, the most important is food. Since the inmate is without many of the amenities that the free man takes for granted, he becomes extremely sensitive to the quality of his diet. It is then not by chance that only the establishment's staff and the prisoners in protection received hot and varied meals at the time of my visits to the penitentiary.

And again,

> It is necessary to state that since 25 July the prisoners in Archambault have been subject to the 'goodwill' of the penitentiaries alone. On the respect of the right to a defence and the right to counsel... in effect, during the time that the Pen was isolated from the rest of the city, all the guarantees pertaining to the right to a full and complete defence were SUSPENDED. To be quite clear on this point, the accused and future accused were handed over DEFENCELESS to the colleagues of the murdered guards and to the Québec Police Force, and were kept HIDDEN for almost three weeks.
>
> ...at the time of this enquiry I can only consider that there EXISTS NO RIGHT TO SEE A LAWYER, only a mere TOLERANCE... The Declaration of the Protection of all Persons against Cruel, Inhuman or Degrading Punishments or Treatments, adopted by the General Assembly of the United Nations, December 9, 1975, which is of higher authority than Canada's own internal law, defines torture as 'any act through which intense physical or mental pain or suffering are deliberately inflicted upon a person by members of the public service, or at their instigation, in order to obtain... information or confessions'... Torture constitutes an aggravated and deliberate form of cruel, inhuman or degrading punishment or treatment.

The Maleville Report concluded that

> ...the methods employed at Archambault since July 26, 1982, clearly constitute the character of torture and cruel, inhuman or degrading punishment or treatment.

The Recommendations must be read in full, to appreciate the quality of this investigation and its positive contribution:

- *The principle of the rule of law must prevail inside Canadian penitentiaries.*

- *The Correctional Investigator must be responsible to Parliament and not to the Solicitor-General.*

- *The penitentiary system must be administered openly and be subject to the control of the citizenry.*

- *Canada must immediately cease its violation of international agreements and its internal legislation.*

- *Canada must be considered to have shown contempt for human dignity and to have denied the objectives of the United Nations Charter.*

- *Canada must be considered guilty of violations of basic human rights and freedoms.*

- *The International Federation of Human Rights must do all in its power to put an end to this situation and keep the United Nations informed on this matter.*

Although Amnesty International had been invited at the same time as the Washington and Paris-based organisations, it was not until many months later in April of 1983 that their investigative committee arrived from London. This marked only the second occasion that Amnesty International has come to Canada — the first being in 1976 when Leonard Peltier, a Native American Indian, was being unjustly extradited from Oakalla, a Canadian prison, where he also was said to have been ill-treated. Amnesty International, however, went on to the U.S. to follow Mr. Peltier's trial and incarceration and filed their report accordingly, omitting any inclusion of the Canadian Government's record of irresponsibility in that matter.

In Amnesty International's report on the Archambault affair, the following excerpts are worthy of note:

> Several prison records were not immediately available... were promised... some were sent later, and *some were not*. (Emphasis added)
>
> Correctional Service regulations require that prisoners be permitted to take showers as soon as practicable after exposure to [tear] gas. No showers were permitted for at least a week following [its] general use...
>
> Fifteen prisoners complained... that they were not permitted to have toilet paper.
>
> Director LeMarier admitted there had been 'regrettable acts committed against the prisoners... that this was a war situation in which a fellow soldier had fallen... it was impossible for me to control the violence and the natural and normal reaction of the guards in the face of the murderous violence of the prisoners; these are feelings of uncontrollable vengeance.'
>
> It is clear that there has been no official investigation of the allegations of ill-treatment.
>
> The Solicitor-General's apparent approach to the allegations... has been to try to pinpoint seeming discrepancies... in an attempt to discredit those who made [them].
>
> Correctional Investigator R.L. Stewart *did* receive a copy of the Kolb Report, but was not asked to nor did he comment on it... *did not* receive copies of the other two outside reports (Maleville and MacDonald).
>
> Every use of force by a Correctional Officer must be recorded on a form pursuant to C.S.C. regulations. The prison was not complying with the regulation.
>
> More recently, the Solicitor-General ordered an independent investigation of allegations that there had been entertainment, including nude dancing, in a prison. It seems odd that the Canadian Government has not initiated a full, independent impartial inquiry into the much more serious allegations which are said to have occurred in the late summer of 1982 at Archambault.
>
> On November 22, 1982, the Solicitor-General seemed quite open to a dialogue. At a second meeting in December he indicated that a public inquiry was out of the question.

On January 6, 1983, Reverend MacDonald sent the Solicitor-General a telex indicating that he had interviewed five prisoners and 'the allegations of harassment and intimidation etc... had been largely substantiated by first-hand information provided by the prisoners... in some cases capable of identifying the guards.' The Solicitor-General has never responded and thus has never seen the notes taken of the five prisoners interviewed.

Prisoners were deprived of all writing materials for several weeks after the riot. Requests... refused by guards. When they began to receive same, some did write complaints but these disappeared after being given to guards.

In January 1983, lawyer Renée Millette submitted written complaints from seventeen individual prisoners to Amnesty International and to two judges in Québec, and in May submitted a complaint to the Attorney-General of Québec requesting an investigation. Judges refused to accept the complaint even for filing....

## Recommendations and Conclusions:

● *Prisoners should have regular access to a doctor and an immediate examination on complaint of ill-treatment... should be a thorough medical examination before being placed in and after being released from segregation.*

● *...mandatory that C.S.C. employees wear name identification on their outer clothing while on duty.*

● *...all prisoners be allowed regular access to a lawyer of his/her choice.*

● *that the Canadian government make widely and forcefully known that the government condemns and will not permit prisoners to be subjected to torture or other cruel, inhuman or degrading treatment or punishment.*

● *...provisions against detention incommunicado, granting... doctors, lawyers and family members access to detainees.*

● *The position of the Solicitor-General that there must be a formal complaint to the courts in order for the authorities to undertake an investigation of the allegations of ill-treatment contravenes Article 9 of the Torture Declaration which states: 'Whenever there is reasonable ground to believe that an act of torture as defined in Article 1 has been committed, the competent authorities of the State shall promptly proceed to an impartial investigation* even if there has been no formal complaint'. (Emphasis added)

● *Amnesty International found that there exists at least reasonable ground to believe that there was, within the meaning of the U.N. Declaration, 'torture or other cruel, inhuman or degrading treatment or punishment' in Archambault Institution during the period beginning 26 July 1982.*

● *The Canadian Government has an international obligation to undertake a full, independent and impartial investigation (which should be made public).*

It is interesting to note here that on the one hand, Amnesty International apparently confirmed many of the torture stories, yet they concluded that there was not *necessarily* torture. As a result of their findings, they informed the Canadian Government of its duty to conduct an investigation, but, in effect, with no accountability or enforcing measures in place. In any event, Canada now rates, for the first time, a dishonourable mention in Amnesty International's 1984 annual report, which lists the growing number of nations requiring investigation into alleged torture of prisoners.

In a similar situation in the Republic of Ireland, Amnesty International released a report in 1978 dealing with maltreatment of prisoners in which they called for a full, impartial and public inquiry. Like the Canadian Government, the Irish Minister for Justice appointed his own committee of inquiry to consider "...what additional safeguards are necessary for the protection against ill-treatment of persons in Garda custody, and the protection of its members... against unfounded allegations of such ill-treatment and that allegations of maltreatment should be investigated through the normal procedure of the courts."

In June of 1983, Amnesty International submitted a private memorandum in which they offered to withhold release of their report until the Canadian Government responded to it. A month later, the Solicitor-General stated that he had requested the Correctional Investigator, *in accordance with his mandate*, to undertake a full investigation.... We find that the Correctional Investigator, R.L. Stewart, was appointed by an order-in-council in 1977 and according to his 'mandate' he is required to "...investigate *on his own initiative*, on request from the Solicitor-General, or on complaint from or *on behalf of inmates as defined in the Penitentiary Act* and report upon problems of inmates that come within the responsibility of the Solicitor General." (Emphasis added)

When requested to carry out a "full, independent and impartial investigation," Stewart's reply indicated his own concern "about maintaining an independent stance," and that he wished to "change the reporting function of [his] position from the Solicitor-General to parliament... as a true ombudsman... [but] to date there has been no movement towards implementation of that change."

Had the Correctional Investigator rejected the request to investigate for the above reason, his image would have been greatly enhanced. Almost a full year after the Archambault incident he still had not initiated an investigation, and by his own admission, his role could hardly be construed as 'independent'. The view has been expressed that the only way a truly independent, impartial inquiry could possibly have been undertaken would have been if Stewart had refused the appointment, clearing the way for a more credible investigation.

According to Amnesty International, the complaints procedure should reflect the following principles, in part: "the investigation body, however constituted, should be able to demonstrate its formal *independence* from the detaining and interrogating authorities as well as from government pressure and influence; and [it] should be capable of acting *on its own initiative*, without having to receive formal complaints, whenever there is good reason to believe that torture has occurred..." (*Torture in the Eighties*, Amnesty International Report, 1984).

In addition, since the Amnesty International Report itself quoted extensively from the Kolb, Maleville and MacDonald investigations, Stewart could have at the very least registered some critical comments in his acceptance of the Solicitor-General's observation: "The Amnesty International Memorandum... describes the allegations in greater detail than has been provided previously... and for the first time documentation from some of the inmates." Apparently the Solicitor-General had still to read Rev. MacDonald's painful interviews with the five Archambault prisoners in January of 1983.

As it developed, the Correctional Investigator's report was not tabled with the Solicitor-General until June 21, 1984, two years after the incident. The Solicitor-General, in turn, released the report on July 9, 1984, the very day of the call for a federal election.

Known as the *Report on Allegations of Mistreatment of Inmates at Archambault Institution Following the Events Which Occurred on July 25, 1982,* some of the more salient features of Stewart's report are listed below:

> *Disappearance of Detention Log Books and Daily Detention Reports:*
> During the course of the investigation two types of records directly relating to the detention unit could not be found for the period in question... A Board of Enquiry was established by the present Warden on August 8, 1983, fourteen months later.... A report was produced in two days. Missing were the detention log books from April 26, 1981, to December 12, 1982, and daily detention reports from June 3, 1982, to January 4, 1983.... no question that these documents contained information vital to this investigation and not available from other sources.... would have identified by name all... officers entering the detention unit and all inmates there at any given time.... had to rely upon the recollection of those officers who did testify, *which was vague and imperfect.*
>
> None of the witnesses called... could account for the disappearance... which appears to suggest that these records might have been *inadvertently destroyed.*
>
> Although the cause of their disappearance remains a matter of speculation, the coincidental disappearance of the only institutional records which would have established the presence of the... staff in the detention unit on a daily basis during the relevant period *suggests that their disappearance was not altogether inadvertent.* (Emphasis added)
>
> *Evidence as to Fabrication and Conspiracy* (among prisoners testifying):
> In May of 1984 the Correctional Investigator received two letters from an inmate who had testified before us in the fall in which he asserted that all of the allegations of mistreatment made by him had been fabricated... There

does exist reliable corroborative evidence that some mistreatment of inmates in detention did take place in July-August 1982, the extent and magnitude of such mistreatment cannot, however, be established.

*Allegations of Mistreatment in the Detention Unit:*

All allegations of mistreatment where a specific guard was identified were, with one exception, denied by the guard in question. No reports relative to the use of force or use of gas were found in the records of the institution. The exception referred to relates to two incidents of humiliating treatment by one guard with respect to one inmate who died prior to this investigation....

*Use of Gas:*

Save the above incidents, no conclusion can be drawn to the occurrence of any specific incident of mistreatment involving a specific guard.

According to the institution, no [tear] gas could be obtained from the armoury without the authorisation of a CX-8 officer. However, the institution could not account for the use of the four partially empty 'deputies' (small aerosol containers). Such rather lax record-keeping shows a clear lack of control of gas inventories.

However, positive testimony was received that gas was in effect used in the detention unit on a number of occasions although the particulars of these incidents cannot be ascertained.

*Alleged Physical Mistreatment on Escorts:*

Evidence suggests that some harassment on the part of the guards occurred. It is quite likely that inmates were harassed physically during escorts, and two guards may have made inordinate use of their riot sticks, although these allegations were denied by the guards. As to the instance of the inmate who alleged he suffered particularly serious mistreatment, this incident represents one of the few incidents where the evidence does confirm that serious physical mistreatment did in fact occur. However, the guard who admitted having escorted this inmate did not remember who the other guards in the escort were, and denied the allegations.

*Alleged Mistreatment in the Cells or Range of Detention Unit:*

Some inmates alleged that the clothing they were given was either soiled or wet, and that mattresses and bedding were soiled and wet, in some cases, with urine. Three guards recalled seeing at least one inmate naked in his cell, but did not take any action to establish why.

It is quite likely that some were kept naked in their cells for some periods, and given the laxness of the guards, the other allegations may not be unfounded. Many of the guards who testified were rather vague in their answers.

Alleged improper conduct on the part of the guards also included being scalded with hot water in the showers; being forced out of the shower with a type of electric prod; being sprinkled with Spic & Span; and being forced out of the shower still covered with soap. And, having his head pushed into his toilet, into human excrement; having testicles squeezed during beatings; being threatened with a knife; and being forced to stand or sit on, or crawl under their beds at night to prevent them from sleeping. Some complained, too, that ropes of bedsheets were placed around their necks and guards threatened to hang them.

No conclusions can be made as to the actual occurrence of any specific instances involving particular guards because of the denial of the guards accused and the lack of sufficient corroborative evidence.

Two inmates alleged to have been sexually harassed. Naked, one was forced to assume various sexual positions, masturbate, and swallow his sperm.

*Alleged Mistreatment in the Yard of the Detention Unit:*

With reference to the allegations of physical mistreatment such as humiliating treatment, sexual harassment and physical threats, any conclusions as to whether such mistreatment did or did not occur is even more difficult to draw due to the fact that by their very nature, they would not leave any physical evidence of their happening. However, if these complaints had been made to physicians, they would have *undoubtedly* seen such physical injuries during their examinations and such would have been noted in their reports.

It is noteworthy that the inmate who was alleged to have suffered sexual harassment did not make any allegations in this respect during his testimony. One would think that such an incident would not have been omitted by this inmate during testimony. (Emphasis added)

Apparently R.L. Stewart didn't get as far as page five of the Amnesty International Report, which explains "...shortly after being subjected to torture or serious ill-treatment, it is often the case that prisoners feel so personally degraded and fearful that they have difficulty admitting that they have been brutally treated — particularly if there is sexual or degrading abuse. Later, when the prisoner is no longer fearful, no longer isolated, and hears that others have been ill-treated, the prisoner may begin to talk more freely, and may even exaggerate the experiences out of desire for revenge."

Nor does Mr. Stewart seem to be familiar with the mass media which is rife with similar examples concerning women who have been sexually assaulted. These fictional characters also demonstrate a pattern of reticence and withdrawal, with disclosures occurring only gradually as the victim begins to feel safe.

*Comments as to the Guards' Testimony as a Whole:*
The majority of the allegations of mistreatment related to a small number of guards. The guards' most common response was 'everything was normal', or, 'I don't remember'. The impression left by the demeanour and response of many guards was simply that they were not forthcoming. Given the circumstances, it is concluded that the majority of the guards put forth a not altogether accurate account. The fact that they were questioned on events which had occurred over one year prior to the investigation can serve to explain to some extent their lack of recall. [Mr. Stewart did not act expediently inasmuch as the investigation was postponed until one year after the fact.] It is certainly reasonable to assume that most of the guards would be shocked and upset and that some would react with a certain degree of bitterness, aggressiveness and animosity towards the inmates.

Why, then, were the guards not immediately transferred?
On August 5th, a group of lawyers associated with La Ligue des Droits et Libertés issued a press release stating that "a

certain number of prisoners have been taken to the hole where they have been the object of particularly cruel treatment... being gassed two or three times a day for five days...."

> *Response by Those in Authority at the Institution:*
> The Commissioner did not recall it being brought to his attention at the time. Newspaper and other reports should have alerted the Warden and the Commissioner that all was not well.... Also, a telex was sent by Professor Georges Lebel of the Association of Québec Jurists which stated "these treatments are inhuman and confirm moral and physical torture in grave violation of constitutional guarantees...." The Warden and the Commissioner acknowledged seeing the telex but did not take any action thereon. Further, *the Commissioner flatly asserted that he had little faith in the credibility of statements issued by the lawyers associated with La Ligue des Droits et Libertés at the time, and as a result, took no action.*
> It is incumbent on the warden and officers in charge to ensure the safety and security of inmates, and not to await specific complaints by specific inmates. (Emphasis added)

One must also question the role of the Correctional Investigator himself, in this regard.

> *The Health Care Unit:*
> Penitentiary Service Regulations require that 'every inmate should be provided, in accordance with the directives, with the essential medical and dental care that he requires.' It is interesting to note that while the institution physician testified that he regularly visited the detention unit every fifteen days, one Health Care Officer testified that it was only on rare occasions, and the Senior Health Officer asserted that the physician visited at least once a month during the relevant period.
> It is difficult to appreciate how an examination could be adequately conducted through the peep hole or the food slot of a closed cell door in close proximity of guards who could overhear any conversation between the inmate and health care officer, especially if the inmates had just suffered some physical mistreatment at the hands of these

same guards. The inmates insisted that they did not complain precisely because of the presence of the guards — three, or as many as six, in one instance.

*Although medical records for the relevant time period were requested, a number were not produced.* (Emphasis added)

## Recommendations:

- *That the use of cells without a supply of water and proper toilet facilities be discontinued, and that all inmates in dissociation be supplied with a mattress and bedding on a twenty-four hour a day basis regardless of the reason for that detention.*

- *That a Health Care Officer visit each occupied cell in dissociation on a daily basis and speak with each inmate without a guard being present, and that he be taken to hospital and given a physical examination if he might have been mistreated.*

- *That accurate and intelligible [tear] gas inventories be kept and staff indicate in writing the purpose and place of use, and that Health Care Officers be thoroughly instructed concerning post-gassing procedures.*

- *That dissociation logs and other original documentation be secured at all times, and that during an emergency situation, an accurate record of work assignments be kept.*

- *That in those instances where an inmate is suspected of being involved in any incident being investigated by the police, and which may lead to criminal charges, he be allowed to consult with counsel prior to being questioned by the police and that he be allowed to have counsel present during such questioning.*

- *That inmates suspected of being involved in serious incidents be removed to other institutions as quickly as possible. [No recommendation is made to remove the guards who are involved.]*

- *And it is essential that there be meaningful attitudinal changes and improvements that come from the administration and filter down to all levels.*

It is important to keep in mind that Stewart did not conduct the inquiry until requested to do so by the Solicitor-General, who in turn did not do so until pressured by Amnesty International. Although Stewart's mandate specifically empowered him to launch the inquiry on his own initiative, not only did he fail to invoke it, but the long delay of a full year tends to reduce its chances for accuracy.

Despite these obstacles, a certain amount of evidence regarding physical brutality was cited, and other similar data could not be denied. The mysterious 'loss' of vital logs, detention centre unit reports, and even medical files, combined to leave the impression that much was awash in the halls of Archambault. In spite of the continued reluctance on the part of the authorities to investigate the 1982 Archambault riot, the Correctional Investigator nevertheless verified the practice of torture, as it is defined in international treaties that Canada has ratified. The term was studiously avoided in Mr. Stewart's report, although he provides documented evidence on page 183: "...at least one inmate was physically mistreated by officers either on escort or in detention, causing him physical injuries...."

Close to two years later, tensions continue to escalate at Archambault and elsewhere on the prison scene. In *Torture in the Eighties*, Amnesty International tells us that "since it is governments that are responsible for torture... and ill-treatment, only governments can in the end effectively prevent it... if they seriously wish to...."

In my view, governments by their very structure must maintain control. 'Wishes' are irrelevant.

\* \* \*

The seeds of the Archambault Theatre Group were planted in the fall of 1976, a time when "something had radically changed... transformed faces, open faces, smiles, hands reaching out. A sparkle in the eyes, something that couldn't be mistaken, something called pride and solidarity. That was the greatest gain of the four-month strike started a year earlier by 400 men who had collectively resolved to take hold of their destinies." (From Paul Rose's Preface to *No Big Deal*, 1978)

The seeds sprouted in February of 1977, a year in which there was an average of one murder every two months at Archambault.

In September of the same year, prior to a planned performance for prison staff of an eight-act play involving dozens of actors, musicians, technicians, artists and writers, the Group was cut down. It had just begun to blossom. "The academic goal had been achieved," said the Administration.

But the roots were not totally destroyed. The play, *No Big Deal*, found its way into the world in book form. Published by Exile Publishers in 1982, the book describes admirably the struggles of the Group, most of whom had no related experience. Against a host of officials who would have preferred that they do their time in a less bothersome way, the camaraderie and coöperation of the prisoners were irrepressible.

The four-month Archambault work strike is the context in which the play takes place. With humour and clarity, the characters depict the maddening frustrations of life in the Pen, as well as cunningly exposing the psychological games played by almost everyone on the 'inside'.

That this play was written and produced in a most repressive and stultifying environment pays tribute to the intelligence and perseverance of those who made it happen. They proved that even under adverse conditions and with very diverse backgrounds, people *can* coöperate, *can* work together peacefully and effectively toward a common goal.

The Administration's decision to terminate the Archambault Theatre Group makes a farce of 'rehabilitation'. Considering the content of the play, it is little wonder that the officials did not want the message of the Group to reach the outside.

> When the sun goes down on Archambault
> I climb in bed and try and sleep.
> Your screws are there to herd my sheep
> And finish off their hard day's load.
>
> Counting us? There's nothing to it.
> They open their book and check right through it.
> Man can't even beat his meat
> Without a cop standing at his feet.

("Archambault". Words and music: Réjean Ferland, *No Big Deal*, 1982)

# Millhaven

> Imprisonment is more than a punishment. It creates a
> new society, the society of the captive. Whereas liberty
> engenders democratic thinking, captivity produces par-
> anoid thinking. (Bruno M. Cormier, M.D.)

Millhaven Maximum Security Penitentiary, a half-hour drive
from Kingston and similar in architectural design to Archambault, opened prematurely in 1971 to accommodate the transfer
of prisoners from the Kingston Pen, which had been the scene
of a grisly riot. Six hundred prisoners had seized control of
the building, with the violence resulting in two deaths and
fourteen sex offenders mutilated.

The following years saw several incidents of violence and
murder at Millhaven, and continual complaints from the prisoners. By the end of 1975, the Report of the Study Group on
Dissociation (November 3, 1975) had:

> ...established beyond question that inmates have, from
> time to time, been restrained by being handcuffed behind
> their backs, shackled with their legs bent backwards and
> upwards in order that the chain between the legs could
> be pulled through the chain on the handcuffs. It was also
> established that inmates had been left in their cells for
> hours in this position and a number of officers agreed
> that they had witnessed inmates lying in their own ex-
> crement. When questioned about these methods of re-
> straint, the Director of Millhaven Institution [later to be
> the first director of Kent Maximum Security in B.C.]
> stated that he was not aware that this was taking place.

In April 1984, an open letter had been forwarded by the
Millhaven Inmate Committee to Dr. Vantour, chairperson of
the Study Group on Murders and Assaults in the Ontario
Region, and to six top prison officials, describing the archetypal
behaviour of guards:

> Since the beginning of this current lockdown situation
> there has been a small group of guards who are acting

as 'agitators' and 'agents provocateurs' in a deliberate effort to further destabilise an already tense situation — the same core who were identified in 1977 by the Parliamentary Subcommittee as participating in an overtime racket which was accomplished through a series of assaults and extortions against fellow guards and inmates alike. They have returned with a vengeance... exploiting the current situation... motives are clear: a further justification for more security measures, which translates into more overtime and more money...

In the disassociation cells, the use of teargas, clubs and mace are becoming commonplace... kicking doors of targetted prisoners at night.... Currently there are approximately forty to fifty in solitary confinement with no charges. There is no need for the stress and anguish caused by these frequent 'round-ups'.

Of the five officers in charge of N-Control, four are members of the conspiracy. We ask if this is just a coincidence... and that you review job assignment sheets to see what, if any, manipulations have been made. We request a full and independent inquiry into our allegations with emphasis on the situation in S.H.U. [Special Handling Unit] and the disassociation cells.

This kind of action coming from the guards is not unusual. After the 1976 B.C. Pen hostage-taking, a prisoner explained in court how the riot was, for the most part, of the guards' own making. Their union was in negotiations, and they needed justification for improved working conditions, higher pay, and more overtime.

The C.S.C. spokesperson insisted that prisoners were free to lay charges against any guards who had assaulted them. This, two years after the same offer was made to the Archambault prisoners who were denied access even to their lawyers for the first ten days into their post-riot scene.

A case in point is that of P.B., who claimed to have been assaulted by six guards at Edmonton Maximum Penitentiary. His bruised condition was testified to by a representative of the Alberta Human Rights Commission. When the prisoner demanded a police investigation, he was interviewed for five minutes, but his witnesses were rejected. The police asked only, "Are they Indians too?" and advised him that he could institute a civil suit, costing approximately $10,000. He was then speedily transferred to another region before his appointment with a Justice of the Peace could be kept in order to lay charges. Despite his general population status, he was forcibly transferred to a Protective Custody Unit. This places a prisoner's life in jeopardy as the news of his location spreads. He received notice of his projected transfer dated *two days after he had already been transferred*. And still we hear the refrain: 'prisoners are free to lay charges against any guards...'

In his Report of the Study Group on Murders & Assaults in the Ontario Region (May 18, 1984), Dr. Vantour may have been reassured that "there is no indication that the Service has refused protection to an inmate who genuinely requires it." However, he displayed a lack of knowledge about cases where prisoners *refuse* such protection, but are still forcibly detained in P.C.U.

Lawyers have also found themselves in untenable positions. Two barristers from the Queen's University Faculty of Law, who were invited to assist in negotiating a peaceful solution to a hostage-taking by prisoners at Millhaven in 1977, left the prison approximately ten hours later after a mutually satisfactory agreement had been reached. They were then advised by the Solicitor-General that the agreement could not be honoured because of the 'no deals' rule recommended by the MacGuigan Subcommittee Report, namely, that no agreements would be negotiated while hostages were being held.

However, the lawyers correctly pointed out that the recommendation was that 'no agreements will be negotiated,' *not* that agreements will be negotiated and then repudiated. They reacted accordingly, issuing a press release, stating in part:

> We can only regard this action as a most serious breach of faith... in this particular case what was agreed upon was so eminently reasonable... acceptable to everyone concerned... that the question of duress should not even arise. The Solicitor-General's action constitutes an unpardonable breach of faith with us... compromising both the obligations and the professional reliance and trust

that were placed in us... an action which must inevitably
breed cynicism and mistrust....

The Solicitor-General remained adamant.

When the 1984 Vantour study was undertaken, violence in
the Ontario region between January 1, 1983, and March 31,
1984, had resulted in thirteen prisoners killed and twenty-
three assaults. The study was to "formulate a series of proposals
which will reduce the likelihood of inmate (and staff) victim-
isation in the future." Other formulations of this report need
to be evaluated in the light of its questionable insight into the
day-to-day problems facing prisoners and staff alike.

Recommendation No. 8 urges "...that the rate of movement
of inmates through the system has to be slowed down in order
to reduce tensions..." This is extremely understated as it is
one of the most tension-producing features of prison life. Forced,
involuntary transfers and their constant threat are most "de-
structive to... the stability [of] the inmate community" and
are a major contribution to the violence which is being
investigated.

Not even in the Correctional Investigator's (C.I.) Annual
Report is a distinction made in the statistical tables between
the voluntary and involuntary type of transfer. When Recommendation 13 ensures "...that correctional officers are as-
signed to specific units for a period of time that will permit
staff and inmates to get to know one another..." it ignores the
Report's own statistics. Annual Reports of the C.I. show that
transfers consistently head the list of unresolved complaints:

| C.I. Ann. Report | Rec'd. | Pending | TOTAL | Resolved | Assisted (visit/ advise) | Unre- solved | TOTAL UNRE- SOLVED |
|---|---|---|---|---|---|---|---|
| 1980-81 | 221 | 20 | 241 | 2 | 9 | 230 | 239 |
| 1981-82 | 234 | 19 | 253 | 0 | 16 | 237 | 253 |
| 1982-83 | 293 | 17 | 310 | 3 | 113 | 194 | 307 |

Many prisoners do not register their complaints with the
C.I., for a variety of reasons, ranging from cynicism to mistrust.

C.G. Rutter, former Director of Inmate Affairs, explained it this way:

> Inmates feared retribution for grieving. And this is a fact. I know this. Do not ask me to prove it. I know. So many things happened that [are] so coincidental to things that did happen after an inmate grieved. (*Minutes of Proceedings*, Issue No. 3, November 3, 1976)

This information was recorded in *Barred from Prison* in 1979 and has never been disputed.

Under the guise of 'administrative' and 'security' reasons, the investigators fail to address themselves to the serious ramifications of forced transfers.

Reference is occasionally made to the expedience of provincial medical health acts which approve the transfer of prisoners to psychiatric wards as their release dates approach, thereby incarcerating them indefinitely, until the pleasure of the Lieutenant-Governor can be prevailed upon to set them free. More terrifying still is Section 545 of the Criminal Code of Canada which authorises the transfer of a prisoner to a mental hospital if 'deemed feeble-minded, insane or imbalanced while in prison.' "Maybe it's the handle to protecting society from some of the very dangerous people," the Solicitor-General was quoted as saying in *The Gazette*, Montréal, in August 1982.

In pursuing the causes of the prevailing violence in Canadian prisons, the Vantour Report also notes that "violence... [can] be seen as a response to tension." More significant is the fact that violence perpetuates tensions, and that includes violence on the part of the keepers as well as that of the prisoners, another factor which was overlooked.

If we are to accept the Report's version of the *laissez-faire* syndrome, that "prisons are effectively run by the prisoners, [and] correctional officers are content to enforce self-protective regulations without effectively protecting prisoners from one another," let us not lose sight of the far more pervasive security measures which are reinforced by goon squads, dogs, police, the military, and the guards' reckless use of firearms. On Page 51 of the Report, we read that "it is recognised that more inmates carry weapons out of fear (self-defence)." Of the 90%

of prisoners suspected of packing 'shivs' in the yard, probably 89% are packing them for self-defence. The justification for threatening them with a recommendation to S.H.U.? — "It's the only way I know to keep them from killing each other," one harassed Warden explained.

While the *laissez-faire* syndrome is applied to the prisoners, why is there no similar definition of the guards, with their increased use of gas, clubs and beatings?

The point is made that "many of the inmates reach C.S.C. with backgrounds of frustration and hatred, lacking communication skills and the ability to solve problems in a verbal, non-violent manner. Violence has become a way of removing problems or a means of expressing frustrations. The main justification for isolating citizens." The insight — that by isolating and not helping prisoners, their frustrations and the threat to the community when they are eventually released are compounded — is not offered.

Unless, of course, there are hidden plans afoot to ensure that some offenders will *never* be returned to society. The Mandatory Supervision (M.S.) parole procedure is an example. Prior to 1970, when prisoners completed their sentence (less one-third off for good behaviour during incarceration, referred to as their remission time), they were automatically released — free. The new Mandatory regulation simply places them under the National Parole Board for this same last third period, thereby effectively retaining control of the individual and negating its original intent.

The Mandatory Supervision system is not working, has not worked, and never will work. During this phase of adverse economic conditions in Canada, about 70% of all persons released solely as a result of M.S. are being returned to the penitentiary, but only about 17% of that number are returned for new criminal charges. The remainder are returned for violations of the term(s) and condition(s) of their M.S. release; for example — *suspicion* of a breach of term or condition, or to *prevent* a breach of term or condition. A prisoner on M.S. may be suspended and/or revoked from liberty for such an unconscionable reason as sitting at a restaurant table with another convicted person.

105

Already, the new Solicitor-General has vowed "either to restrict the Mandatory Supervision system, or abolish it completely... prefer[ring] to abolish it" (*Vancouver Sun*, November 6, 1984). An important factor which is overlooked is that by wiping out good time (remission), there is little incentive for prisoners to follow the rules and regulations. Thus already troubled Wardens would have more difficulty 'controlling' their charges.

In the same news release, University of British Columbia law professor Michael Jackson puts forward the consideration that "the government seems to be reacting to a few highly publicised examples of convicts on mandatory supervision who commit new crimes." And of even greater importance is that the Solicitor-General's plan would "deprive many people of their liberty who are never going to commit another crime."

In 1983, another procedure, called 'gating', was initiated. Prisoners whom the National Parole Board considers (with no supportive legal evidence necessary) to be potentially dangerous when released on M.S. are immediately returned the moment they step outside the gates. "It hasn't worked. A man's sentence should end, period," insists an officer of the St. Leonard Society of Halfway Houses who has consistently opposed Mandatory Supervision.

Again, like so many other government reports, the Vantour Report attempts to deal with areas of violence as isolated phenomena, rather than seeing violence as inherent in the prison system. To do otherwise would mean that they would have to draw the conclusion that no amount of patching up could detract from the firm fact that prisons provide *no* adequate solutions either to deterring crime or for protecting society.

As Canada joins the international community in demanding the preservation of human rights for victims of military dictatorships, it comes as a surprise to find the Vantour Report appearing to regret "the growing influence of the 'rights' movement with its pressures to 'liberalise' or 'normalise' institutions so that they more closely approximate life on the outside." Ontario Regional Coroner Robert McMillan, quoted in the Kingston *Whig Standard*, March 21, 1984, also "points to an increasing recognition of prisoners' legal rights as another source of trouble inside prisons."

It is no great revelation that such sentiments are held by responsible people in a society which purports that the rule of law applies to all citizens.

The reference to the proliferation of "independent watchdogs such as the Correctional Investigator, Independent Chairperson, Inspector-General, Director of Inmate Affairs, and an elaborate grievance procedure — the end product is a system characterised by justice or fairness and thus accountability," is questionable also. How employees appointed by the C.S.C. can be considered 'independent watchdogs' defies all logic. Accountability can be meaningful only when it involves being answerable to the public — no more, no less.

Regarding the Inmate Committee, the Report states that it "may be of shorter duration than previously, so much so that by the time an Inmate Committee election has taken place, some of the candidates have been transferred." It conveniently fails to investigate the possible reasons for this modification — that an Inmate Committee member who shows too great a sense of responsibility and efficiency is seen as a threat to 'the good order of the institution' and can suddenly find himself or herself transferred. Or when the Warden vetoes the election of a certain prisoner, others refuse to stand for election. It is little wonder that many prisons no longer have an Inmate Committee.

On double-bunking, the Report disposes of prisoners' resistance to it with "inmates' anticipation of the negative effects of double-bunking may have created a self-fulfilling prophecy," which ignores the effects of the invasion of privacy. Forcing anyone to share indefinitely a six-by-eleven-foot space, which includes sharing the toilet, sink, and sleeping facilities in a room equivalent in size to an average apartment bathroom, is to display a most insensitive attitude.

In an astonishing downplay of overcrowding as a contributing factor to tension, the Report says that "...overcrowding may be something that the Service has to live with," but says nothing about how the prisoners must live with it. The Committee further states that they "do not think that our society will tolerate human warehousing," even while prisoners, with little or no meaningful programmes, are being stacked like cordwood, awaiting their release dates.

Inherent in overcrowding or 'warehousing' are reduced recreation and exercise time and the lack of purposeful occupation and job and educational training. While the Report tells us that overcrowding may have to be tolerated, it also tells us that it causes 'enforced idleness' and "that idleness, in part due to overcrowding, is considered a problem...." Happily, the Report does not advocate construction of more prisons, despite the steady increase in the population in existing prisons.

In their examination of the rate of murders and assaults at Millhaven, Collins Bay and Frontenac, the investigators appear to have deviated from the Solicitor-General's statistics when they maintain that "there is no evidence of a significant increase in the proportion of inmates being admitted for crimes of violence [nor] that prison terms are longer (with the exception of sentences for murder convictions)." Addressing the Canadian Bar Association in Winnipeg in September 1984, the Solicitor-General spoke of "...the largest rise in inmate population in Canadian history in any four-year period..." and went on to say:

> Crime itself has not increased significantly and has even decreased in some of the most serious areas like murder. [But] judges are imposing harsher penalties. [There are] far more two- and three-year sentences for matters which would have received provincial time before. [And] at the other end of the sentence, the National Parole Board has significantly reduced its release rate. Most Canadians believe the opposite, that violent crime is increasing and that the courts and Parole Board are becoming more lenient.

In this connection, *The Royal Bank Letter* of May-June 1984 further confirms how Canadians tend to overestimate the incidence of violent crime. In the results of a poll in which Canadians were asked: "In your opinion, of every 100 crimes committed in Canada, what percentage involve violence?, the respondents estimated 53.9%. In fact, the number of crimes of violence in the past few years has amounted to no more than 8% of all offences reported to the police." The letter also touches on how parole "is not granted as freely in Canada as in most other Western countries. The National Parole Board rejects about 60% of all initial applications."

In still another area, the Vantour Report proves itself lamentably ill-informed. When it considers that "inmates' survival methods are those that will ensure their incarceration... in an environment of intimidation and fear, and consequently, ripe for violence," no cognizance is taken of the problems faced by many, particularly lifers, who do try to keep things cool. For example, a prisoner often finds that physical force is required to subdue feuding cellmates, after which he may find himself charged with assault and recommended to S.H.U. One prisoner has faced this kind of situation six times to date. His solution is to turn day into night. In order to keep a low profile and minimise confrontations which inevitably entrap him, he sleeps days and uses the nights to read and write. His method is not unique, but merits attention since few will credit prisoners for their efforts.

The last section of the Report is devoted to the Special Handling Unit at Millhaven, and another in Québec, the combined population of which soared from the original fifty-one in August 1980 to 176 within three months. In 1981 alone, ninety-nine more were approved for transfer. The most definitive study of this area to date is offered by Professor Michael Jackson in his book *Prisoners of Isolation*. It signals a breakthrough in the conspiracy of silence in the face of brutalities committed behind prison walls, from Jackson's general introductory remarks, "...because the prison is the most forceful expression of society's condemnation, it raises the issues of morality of state power in its starkest form..." to the observation of prisoner Jack McCann, who has so far spent a staggering eleven and a half years in solitary confinement:

> All you live on is bitterness and hatred. For some guys that's not enough... their hatred reaches the point when they have to see blood even if it's their own... I have fear of losing my sanity....

Professor Jackson's observations of the Vantour-McReynold Model (1977), with its three-phased programme, takes careful

109

note of the fact that "there is nowhere any provision requiring a hearing at which the prisoner can hear the case against himself or make any representation on his own behalf" — a fundamental right any accused should possess where the rule of law is claimed to exist.

This later Vantour Report makes no mention of this omission, nor does it venture any criticism of the fact that S.H.U. in Québec's Centre de Développement Correctionnel (C.D.C.) "places much greater emphasis on control and prides itself on being 'firm but fair' [and] makes no pretence about the purposes of S.H.U., [namely] to incapacitate 'particularly dangerous criminals'." Neither was there any allusion to Professor Jackson's exposé that "there was no pretence that the phase system had been implemented [at C.D.C.] as it 'boasted' the unusual feature of 'keeping prisoners in cells... under surveillance'" — literally — as officers patrol on top of the cells along specially constructed catwalks, rifles in hand.

In fact, it has to be noted that nowhere in his 115-page Report, which includes a chapter on the Special Handling Unit, does Dr. Vantour draw upon the exhaustive research on the same subject in Michael Jackson's *Prisoners of Isolation*.

Professor Jackson symbolises, in the following passage, the rejected who die in prison:

> As I left the C.D.C.... I was shown the small cemetery located just outside the perimeter fence. It is the burial ground for men who die in the penitentiary and whose bodies are not claimed by relatives. Inscribed on the headstones in this small windswept plot of earth are not the names of the men, but their penitentiary numbers. Reducing a man to nothing but a number and burying him is a far more accurate reflection of the psychological reality of the special handling unit than is the rhetoric of Dr. Vantour's phase programme.

While the Vantour group was "struck by the fact that inmates 'survive' the S.H.U. ordeal" and noted that "they will survive with or without programmes," they obviously had not counted the number of suicides, nor the slash marks up and down the arms of many, nor had they measured the rate of deterioration of their lives, especially following their release back into the community. Reading between the lines, what we see is that some prisoners manage to *outlast* others.

A letter from a prisoner in Millhaven segregation gives us some real insight:

> Do you know a dude called J? They're playing games with him lately. Locked up for no reason. Anyway, J blew all our lights last night by slashing his throat. I felt something was wrong but I never expected that kind of action. J is losing it. He's losing his hate, and without a furious hate, burnout is inevitable. What freaks me out is J and me both got the same amount of time in, on the same beefs. I've had twenty times more lockup time than him. I hope I don't slip into burnout. I'd rather die trying for the fence than by my own hand. But it's nowhere J is coming from. After so much time you say, okay, that's it! I've had enough. I can't take no more time. But no one listens, and the big pig system smiles, as the torture goes on.

When I asked this man during a recent visit how he was managing, he told me not to worry, that he was able to maintain enough hatred for the system to stay alive, since the alternative was to become suicidal. When I wondered was there not some leeway for a measure of love to help him along, he showed surprise at the question. After nine years, looking at minimum 25, the question appeared to make no sense to him at all.

In weighing whether the Special Handling Unit should continue, the Vantour committee was emphatic in its decision that there *should* be one, based upon information gained from "interviews with many who felt that some S.H.U. inmates should and could be returned to regular population [while] others should stay in forever," which hardly reflects a studied scientific approach. Although "recognising the absence of any therapeutic value... and the fact that prolonged periods in segregation with minimum due process safeguards may be considered inhumane," and acknowledging that "the ultimate goal of the criminal justice system is the reintegration of the offender into the community, similarly the ultimate goal of a segregation unit ought to be to return the inmate to association...

111

in a maximum security institution as soon as possible," the Report informs us that they "find the abolition of S.H.U.'s unacceptable if the only alternative is to return the 'particularly dangerous inmates' to a Maximum Security prison population... similarly [we] oppose their return to administrative segregation facilities in Maximum Security prisons."

What they do recommend and emphasise repeatedly is that the Service needs more 'purpose-built' institutions. A euphemism by any other name....

As of October 1984, the last of the Millhaven S.H.U. prisoners were transferred to Saskatchewan Penitentiary in Prince Albert, with its newly constructed Special Handling Unit added to the existing Protective Custody Unit. The two sharing the same compound is a potentially volatile combination, regardless of the separating walls and yards. Moreover, another two such 'purpose-built' S.H.U.'s are scheduled to open shortly. One is located on the grounds of Maximum Security Archambault in Québec, and the other, again, will share facilities with a P.C.U. in remote Renous, New Brunswick. This will bring the total S.H.U. capacity to 240 cells. With the present count at 116 (according to information provided by the Assistant Commissioner of Security's Ottawa office in December 1984), one has to question how many prisoners are likely to be reclassified as 'violent' in order to maintain the 'cost-effectiveness' of the shiny new quarters.

This, then, is their answer to the spate of murders and assaults at Millhaven and other prisons. One can predict with reasonable certainty that such 'purpose-built' prisons will only exacerbate the already overwhelming problems facing the Correctional Service of Canada.

In fact, it is already happening. In the first month of the arrival of Millhaven's S.H.U. occupants at Prince Albert, accounts of their bewilderment and frustration are even now overwhelming. Letters received in October 1984 include the following:

> The meals here are unbelievable. The bare minimum is one tea, one milk, two slices of bread... and the main course. Not enough to feed a cockroach... served in small amounts, just enough to keep us alive and forever hungry.

Every day we have to *stand* for the count, otherwise get charged. They command us to stand by yelling at us and using foul language to intimidate us.

We only get twenty to thirty minutes exercise outside, instead of one hour.

We're being isolated for refusing to give blood, and it clearly states in our Handbook of Inmates' Rights that we may refuse medical treatment.

I'm writing to you from S.H.U. in Saskatchewan. I was charged with [internal] attempted murder, aggravated assault and a weapon charge... went to court and found not guilty of all three charges and was still sent here. Staff told me if I was telling the truth it would come out at court (and it did) and I would not be sent to S.H.U., which was their only reason why I should be sent here. My transfer here can't be justified.

The Prisoners' Rights Group (P.R.G.) has since been informed by the Assistant Commissioner of Security that this case "will be reviewed again in November 1984 since the charges against him were dropped," completely disregarding the fact that he was transferred to S.H.U. *after* his court appearance, when the charges *were* dropped.

Consistent with the ineptitude of our political and economic decision-makers in coping with the basic needs of the majority of Canadian people, the management of the prison system appears to be incapable of operating without the level of harassment calculated to produce more chaos and more destruction.

## Stony Mountain

The prison is obsolete, cannot be reformed, should not be perpetuated through the false hope of forced treatment, and should be repudiated and abandoned. (William G. Nagel)

Overcrowding and double-bunking may be a fairly new feature in Canadian prisons, but that it contributes to increasing

113

tensions can no longer be denied. In 1983 four prisoners at Stony Mountain filed a writ in Federal Court declaring that overcrowding and sharing of cells were in violation of the Charter of Rights "...because they are punitive and deprive prisoners of personal security" (*Globe & Mail*, July 16, 1984). On November 6, 1984, the Federal Court Judge ruled that double-bunking does not subject the inmate to any cruel and unusual treatment or punishment.

The 1983 Joint Statement by the Heads of Correction, titled *Incarceration: A Plea for Restraint*, provides the following statistics relating to overcrowding:

> At the Federal level, since January 1, 1983, penitentiaries have experienced a net increase of 25 inmates a week. In a little less than four months, there is a sufficient increase to fill a new 400-man institution. Over a year this would represent a requirement for 3.25 new 400-man institutions at a cost of $150,000 to $200,000 per cell (1983 estimates) or as much as $80 million per maximum security institution. From another perspective it would require a construction expenditure of $260 million!

And from the *Calgary Herald* (July 23, 1984):

> ...prison population has increased at an average rate of 7% *in each of the past 3 years*, compared with 2.4% *in the previous 40 years*. (Emphasis added)

The *Toronto Star* of August 18, 1984, tells us that:

> In the Federal system alone, nearly 1,000 are double-bunked — two men sharing a cell that is usually 9 by 6 feet. [In Toronto, some city jails are holding four men to a cell.] Canada imprisons 116 per 100,000 [a figure which has not been adjusted since the increase in prison population in the past few years]. This compared with the U.S.A.: 212 per 100,000 — nearly double Canada's rate of incarceration. However, the U.S. has *five* times the rate of violent crime and would therefore be jailing closer to *500* per 100,000 were it imprisoning as many people [proportionately] as Canada.

Despite this evidence, the *Whig-Standard* (July 30, 1984) has the Solicitor-General surprising us with:

> ...double-bunking will cease by August of next year... possibly because the prison population is finally *on the decline*.... figures from the second quarter of 1984 demonstrate *a decrease*.... three new institutions are being built while others that were to be closed will be kept open [and expanded]. (Emphasis added)

More and larger prisons are being built to deal with the overcrowding that is only now reluctantly admitted to be a major source of tension, and to accommodate what all the statistics — except the Solicitor-General's — show to be a snowballing prison population. The satisfaction resulting from jobs created by such expansion is offset by the toll in human misery for those who are to occupy these less than civilised quarters.

The MacGuigan Report to Parliament in 1977 warned that unless its recommendations for reform were implemented there would be continued and increasing violence and chaos in the system. Seven years later, the *Calgary Herald* reported that "vicious outbreaks of rioting, violence and hostage-taking periodically erupt and rip apart the superficial calm of Canada's major prisons... where terror, torture, injury and death can strike with frightening speed as a result of tension, boredom, hate or provocation..." (July 23, 1984).

Stony Mountain is a 107-year-old prison just north of Winnipeg. With a capacity of 478, it has at times held as many as 509 prisoners. Like other vintage Canadian prisons, it has been the scene of many disturbances over the years. Since 1982, when prisoners went on a rampage to protest double-bunking, there have been several attempted hostage-takings and murders of guards as well as prisoners.

On May 19, 1984, a lone prisoner attempted to take a hostage. Ten days later, the entire prison population were still confined to their cells with all their rights suspended. Their complaints to the Solicitor-General of being the victims of vengeance were ignored, and the Assistant Warden defended the lockup as a way to keep order in the prison.

It should have come as no surprise when on July 13 (co-incidentally, four days after the release of the Correctional Investigator's report on Archambault), two guards at Stony Mountain were killed. Four prisoners were charged. The total population was locked up twenty-four hours a day for two weeks, and the Warden admitted (*Globe & Mail*, August 20, 1984) that he was considering permanently restricting recreation and the inmates' freedom to move within the prison.

Steve Fineberg of the Québec-based Prisoners' Rights Committee presented a Brief in September 1984 to the Advisory Committee to the Solicitor-General on *The Management of Correctional Institutions*. It is presented in part here, as it relates to the situation at Stony Mountain, which

> provides an example of repressive Administration reaping its reward. On May 29, the Chairman of the Inmate Welfare Committee wrote to the Solicitor-General to inform him that the entire population was still in deadlock... "I believe it is wrong to punish 500 inmates for the actions of a few. If the Administration thinks, or can prove, that violence is increasing I think they should tell us and we can work together to prevent [it] and clear up the problems. I believe that the Warden's action, locking up the entire population, was a drastic overreaction... irrational, unwarranted and harsh beyond what was required."
>
> The Inmate Welfare Committee went on to detail various acts of repression... including transfers to Maximum and the hole for protesting the deadlock, strip searches, reduction of meals and destruction of inmates' property, including photographs of friends and family... a complaint common among P.R.C.'s clients in Québec [and from east to west across Canada]. "The inmates of this institution feel we are being subjected to a general act of vengeance. Many inmates have lost respect for the Administration and its ability to run the institution in a fair and rational manner. This is a very dangerous situation."
>
> The Warden [had] enunciated his attitude clearly in a May 22 confidential memorandum to all staff: "...In my view we are at present in a perfect position to install new policies and procedures which will improve our level of control of the inmate population... We will take this opportunity to put them into place."

116

The same month at the National Conference of C.S.C. Administrators, Commissioner Yeomans was telling the wardens: "Take control of your institutions. You've got the authority to do that!" (*Let's Talk*, July 30, 1984).

> A further example of illegality is found in the institutional response to the deaths of two guards in July 1984.... The residents of at least one range were assaulted by the Prairie Emergency Response Team, as it led shackled prisoners to the R.C.M.P. for questioning. If no allegations were made publicly in this matter it is out of fear of reprisals. The guards simply waited until they were together with prisoners out of range of the totally inadequate cameras and the members of the C.A.C....
>
> ...the Inmate Committee chairman stated that he "and the other members of the Committee, like all Canadians, are deeply saddened... and are horrified by the violence surrounding the officers' deaths..." adding that a major source of tension was "a series of changes to institutional routine which adversely affect inmate welfare." These changes were made without consulting or even informing inmates. "...at this point the process is either being ignored or is not working." At the time of writing the population was confined to their cells and were not permitted to contact lawyers for a certain period of time following the deaths.
>
> A further statement [to the Solicitor-General] from the Inmate Welfare Committee on August 13th reads: "I told you in May that we were subjected to a general act of vengeance. You have now condoned the act and sent a clear message to all inmates... that we cannot look to you to restore any sense of reason or justice... I do not want to be responsible for any trouble your letter may cause so I will not be releasing it to the population."

The Solicitor-General's letter had stated: "I have no reason to believe that the Warden acted improperly and I fully support his decision to order an institutional lockup and his handling of the entire situation."

What it comes down to, then, are two very different attitudes regarding the management of prisons: one of negotiation and coöperation, the other of confrontation and control. With the

117

previous Administration there *had* been consultation and the process did work. But after the May hostage-taking, the prisoners pointed out that "because certain correction policies may be a cause of institutional tensions [we] feel that only an independent and public inquiry will be able to do the kind of investigation required."

Again there was no response.

Regarding prisoners' rights to see their lawyers and be in contact with the outside world following violent incidents, Fineberg had this to say:

> ...despite the lesson of Archambault, prisoners are still cut off from the outside world following internal incidents. When guards were killed at Stony Mountain, lawyers were prevented from contacting their clients. The Administration claimed the clients were not asking for lawyers' services at this time. Administration should admit that when a penitentiary is shut down, *all* prisoners are fearful and eager to see their lawyers, but are unable to communicate that wish to the outside world. In the case in hand, the *lawyers* who were excluded *possessed standing instructions to meet with the Inmate Welfare Committee* in the event of any incident in the institution. (Emphasis added)

Lawyers from the Public Interest Law Department of Legal Aid, Manitoba, expressed concern to the *Vancouver Sun* (July 24, 1984) that the Administrators were "on a dangerous collision course" and that "no one can be subject to total domination of their lives...." When they asked permission to speak to the inmates' representatives, the Warden claimed, "that would be a provocation at this point" (*Globe & Mail*, July 22, 1984). That repercussions were not limited to prisoners became clear when one Winnipeg lawyer was offered money to stop defending one of the four convicts involved in the murders. He complained that "It's almost like a lynch mob atmosphere out there... let's remember they are innocent until proven guilty." A month after the incident, Legal Aid lawyers still had not received an answer to their call for a thorough investigation.

After the July events at Stony Mountain, a C.B.C. camera crew spotted guards disguised by balaclavas or riot helmets and with plexiglass shields held in front of them. The Warden later admitted to the *Toronto Star* (July 30, 1984) that "an Emergency Response Team had been running the prison." An editorial in the same paper expressed its outrage at such a policy: "...even prisoners deserve the right to know who their jailers are. Prisons are tough and dehumanising enough without a policy that takes away jailers' faces. Even behind bars justice should be open [and] doesn't need to be behind a mask."

An editorial in the *Toronto Star* (July 27, 1984) gives undue credit to the attempts to 'humanise the system' when it refers to trailer family visits, the increased access to psychiatric and other treatment services and the recognition of prisoners' rights. But it omits many of the relevant facts. For example, only twelve of the 450 prisoners at Stony Mountain were initially eligible for family visits, and access to treatment was in reality very inadequate, as is seen in the case of the diabetic prisoner who required regular insulin shots followed by a meal. He was receiving his shots at irregular times followed either by no food, or by contra-indicated jam sandwiches. His requests to see the doctor were either delayed or refused (*Winnipeg Free Press*, August 17, 1984).

According to other reports, the condoning of violence against a prisoner again appeared evident when a doctor diagnosed a prison guard as being "...paranoid, depressed and suspicious of his fellow officers [and] suffering from stress, and... ill." That the guard was 'suffering' is not an unnatural consequence of "putting in more than 100 hours of overtime... to pick up the slack" (and the money) in an atmosphere where a tray for prisoners' grievances is labelled a 'Snivel and Whine Box' (*Winnipeg Free Press*, August 23, 1984).

Further to the 'recognition of prisoners' rights', one Tory M.P., William Van Koughnet, called "for the return of corporal punishment, favour [ing a] wide, wooden or leather paddle administered to bare buttocks... just to teach them a little more respect [for the guards]" (*Globe & Mail*, August 23, 1984).

It is significant that the medical profession should find itself in a dilemma when its first responsibility, even before fulfilling its Hippocratic or Florence Nightingale oaths, is to its employer (the C.S.C.). However, like any other conscientious professional body, it does have the opportunity to redeem itself by exposing policies which violate its medical standards. "...ethically no doctor should ever authorise punitive reductions in diet, exercise or showers... or punitive or administrative segregation," cites the Fineberg brief. "An ex-prisoner tells us of the three occasions when he received the lash as an adolescent; on each occasion it was authorised by a doctor employed by the penitentiary service.... The C.S.C. has not fully consigned that dilemma to the past."

Instead of decreasing the number and length of prison sentences or releasing non-violent offenders at the earliest possible date, the authorities have begun to transfer prisoners from Stony Mountain to other prisons — a move which will not only contribute to overcrowding elsewhere, but one which will also compound the problems of forced involuntary transfers.

To deflect the unfavourable publicity surrounding the Archambault riot, the Solicitor-General made a unique commitment in the House of Commons on November 8, 1982, to call the Correctional Investigator in at once "...if and when an incident of this sort... ever takes place again... to be present as much as possible during the incident and during its aftermath." A fine recommendation were it ever implemented.

In 1980, at Dorchester, the use of violence against prisoners was denied, only to be contradicted by the leaked report of the Inspector-General.

In 1982, the violence against prisoners in the aftermath of the Archambault riot was continually denied despite evidence to the contrary in investigations by three international bodies and one Church Moderator.

In 1984 at Stony Mountain, the continued beatings and ill-treatment of prisoners warrant only the Solicitor-General's comment: "I fully support the Warden's handling of the entire situation...."

To this day, there has been no independent public inquiry into the reprisals against prisoners following the deaths of two guards at Stony Mountain, nor, as far as we can learn, did the Solicitor-General "call in at once the Correctional Investigator to be present as much as possible during the incident and its aftermath."

*Plus ça change, plus c'est la même chose.* (The more things change, the more they stay the same.)

## Renous

> The federal penal system is part of 'big government' —
> one is no better than the other. Prisoners here are largely
> powerless, colonials not citizens. (Daniel Berrigan)

In dire economic times, converting an abandoned ammunition depot into a thriving industry tendering twelve contracts and eventually providing 365 permanent jobs must seem like a godsend. The project is underway deep in the woodlands of New Brunswick, where over half the population has been unemployed for many years. Who would want to turn down a $78 million facility with an annual operating budget of $18.5 million?

Those who would turn it down are already being heard, as Canada's version of Alcatraz comes into view. Situated about 100 miles north of Moncton, Atlantic Institution, Maximum Security-Protective Custody, as it is formally called, or Renous, as it is more commonly referred to, is drawing heated reactions. "If the Liberals want jobs for the area, they could have spent money on a Honda plant," says criminologist Professor Irwin Waller in the *Toronto Star*, July 3, 1984. The same newspaper has Réal Jubinville of the Canadian Association for the Prevention of Crime complaining: "They're literally going to exile hundreds of prisoners... they're out of their minds by going against what every study on the location of prisons has recommended."

This same account goes on to describe how Renous has become the target of critics who say that not only is the location wrong, but "The proposed prisoner composition (S.H.U.-P.C.U.) is explosive, and... its whole concept treats the incarceration and rehabilitation of prisoners as just another industry to be wooed, like an auto factory to an area of high unemployment." Furthermore, the *Whig Standard* (August 13, 1984) has its reporter telling us that "This $78 million prison works out to $228,000 [estimates have since soared to $237,000]

121

per cell. The mortgage on that works out to almost $1 million per month, or another $30,000 [added to the current $50,000] a year for each prisoner, and whatever it will cost a few years down the line to convert it."

Liberal M.P. Maurice Dionne, electioneering in 1980, promised this job creation project as a boost to the economy, and as a ploy to ensure his own re-election. As late as August 19, 1984, while participating in a cornerstone-laying ceremony with the Solicitor-General, who promised the community that all goods and services would be purchased locally whenever possible, Mr. Dionne reminded the audience that penitentiaries never go bankrupt or into receivership, so there would be secure positions. A month later he lost his seat in the House of Commons.

In July 1984, newpapers reported that senior C.S.C. officials had privately admitted they had overestimated the number of Special Handling Units that would be required across Canada by 1986. The human ramifications of this error in calculation are that prisoners will be railroaded into Renous and other S.H.U.'s under construction, by the authorisation of the Commissioner's Directive dealing with those who are *suspected* of being dangerous, *not only* those who are summarily *classified* as being dangerous. It is obvious that many more prisoners, with no avenue for appeal, are being and will continue to be labelled 'violent' at the discretion of the Administration, in order to fulfill this overestimation of the number of cells required.

Even if there is a need to construct another Maximum Security Penitentiary, why is it necessary to build one in remote Renous (population 500)? Renous critics both inside and outside the C.S.C. who ask this question are being ignored entirely. Disregarded also is the 1977 Parliamentary study which concluded that visits by prisoners' families are crucial to their rehabilitation, as their ties with the outside community are vital. Proximity to courts and to legal, medical and educational services was also overlooked.

Renous is clearly a disaster waiting to happen.

If one were to wonder upon what logic the plan was based, some answers could be found in an Official Correctional Service of Canada publication entitled *The Impact of Prison Size on Prison Population*, undated and unsigned, strangely enough. Based on a dispassionate approach which would be more appropriate to a survey of a meat processing plant, it advances such simplistic analyses as "the costs of a Medium Security Institution with a prisoner population of 420 is $12,420 less 'per offender' than one with 168 inmates. Even more dramatic, in a Maximum Security Institution with a population of 428, the savings amount to $19,600 [compared to] an institution with 162 inmates." In addition, the study tells us that large prisons were shown to be more cost effective than small ones, and that "vocational and educational training, individual or group counselling and therapeutic correctional environments have *no appreciable impact on an inmate's prison behavior or future criminality.*" (Emphasis added)

A touching concern is displayed when the study adds "Prisons should be designed so that they are pleasant for the prisoner to live in... with the aim of ensuring that the prisoner suffers only by losing his liberty and not in any other way." That this report may have been prepared in some distant sanctuary, far removed from the reality of prison life, is further suggested by the utterly meaningless passage: "The aim of preventing the offender [from] committing crimes... is one which can be achieved." How this can be achieved is left to the reader's imagination. "Practical help... [for] the prisoner toward the end of his sentence to help with employment, accommodation, financial and family problems... can reduce reconviction rates." Where this help is to come from is not explained.

We are counselled, however, not to worry: "Large institutions are no less effective than small ones and therefore are more practical to build because they are much cheaper to operate..." and "Although treatment programmes have no demonstrable effect on recidivism rates [they do] provide meaningful work for staff and keep inmates occupied."

And finally, the study concludes with this gem: "Overcrowded prisons and common economic sense dictates such a course of action, for in the final analysis, *it helps to bridge the gap between our knowledge and [our] ignorance of human behaviour.*" (Emphasis added)

One must admire the wisdom of leaving the report unsigned.

*  *  *

The foregoing description of the past decade of riots in Canadian prisons was planned to conclude with the ill-omened Renous. However, history moves on.

On August 7, 1984, we were confronted with the "historic decision to build the first Federal penitentiary in Windsor, Newfoundland" (*Toronto Star*). It was to be a $12.5 million Minimum-Maximum facility to house eighty prisoners, and was to create 100 construction jobs followed by sixty permanent prison positions, with an operating budget of $2.5 million and a grant in lieu of taxes. The money was already set aside. It was even going to solve all the double-bunking problems, we were assured. The only reason for the delay was "...in the past... the Federal government has never been able to be certain that there would be any population for a Federal institution once constructed."

The announcement to provide this historic boost to the Newfoundland economy was made a month prior to the September 1984 federal election. It was withdrawn a month later. No reason was offered, just that the deal was off.

One less prison to fill.

St. Vincent-de-Paul Maximum Security Penitentiary near Montréal. (Photo: Radio-Québec)

St. Vincent-de-Paul Maximum Security Penitentiary near Montréal.
(Photo: Radio-Québec)

Troops from C.F.B. Chilliwack prepare for order to move into Matsqui Medium Security Penitentiary, B.C., June 1981. (Photo: Ken Oakes, *The Vancouver Sun*)

Ambulances wait for casualties outside Matsqui Medium Security Penitentiary, B.C., June 1981. (Photo: Ken Oakes, *The Vancouver Sun*)

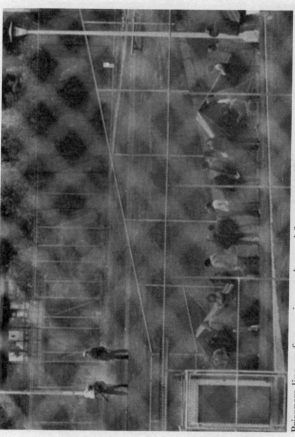

Prisoners line up for evening meal served from a tent following riot at Matsqui Medium Security Penitentiary, B.C., June 1981. (Photo: Ken Oakes, *The Vancouver Sun*)

St. Vincent-de-Paul Maximum Security Penitentiary near Montréal.
(Photo: Radio-Québec)

St. Vincent-de-Paul Maximum Security Penitentiary near Montréal. (Photo: Radio-Québec)

St. Vincent-de-Paul Maximum Security Penitentiary near Montréal. (Photo: Radio-Québec)

# Chapter 3

# Why Prisons?

*Hell hath no fury like a bureaucracy defending itself.*

Tom Wicker

# 3 Why Prisons?

*Imprisonment is slavery. Like slavery, it was imposed on a class of people by those on top. Prisons will fall when their foundation is exposed and destroyed by a movement surging from the bottom up.*

Instead of Prisons, *1976*

## Industry and Control

When you've seen one prison riot you've seen them all — admittedly a flippant commentary on the previous section. Nevertheless, it is difficult to draw any rational conclusion given the consistency with which the signals coming from the prisoners and their committees are so strenuously ignored by officialdom. Even more cynical would be the question: Having outfitted, armed and trained I.E.R.T.'s (Institutional Emergency Response Team — a euphemism for old-fashioned goon squad), must they not be put to use?

In searching for an explanation of the rejection of lessons which beg to be learned, we must understand the vital role which the Criminal Justice System (C.J.S.) plays as a part of state control. Bureaucracies generate their own incompetence, and balance their confusion and even self-destruction against the diabolical success with which they prolong the stay of most prisoners, who are essential for the operation of the prison industry. According to Eckstedt and Griffiths in their recent study, *Corrections in Canada: Policy and Practice*, the Correctional Service of Canada (C.S.C.) employs 10,883 people (excluding outside contracts) as part of the C.J.S., which comprises as well all federal, provincial and municipal courts of law and police forces, and the National Parole Board (N.P.B.). The C.J.S. employs a total of 108, 366 people, of whom 17,015, or more than fifteen per cent, hold administrative positions. The 1979 budget of $2.5 billion is estimated to have reached the $3 billion mark.

A further example of prolonging the containment of the 'merchandise' is provided in sentence computations. When prisoners query their sentence computations, they can often be provided with three different calculations, of which the 'front office' can be depended upon to select the longest period. The 1982-83 annual report of the Correctional Investigator indicates a sharp increase in the number of complaints received regarding 'sentence administration' — ninety-seven, compared to a mere (!) sixty-two in 1980-81. Obviously, one way to deal with the serious overcrowding would be to release all those who are serving time beyond their legal release date — a challenge which has never been accepted by any of the C.S.C. specialists.

Before leaving the prisoner-as-merchandise analogy, serious attention must be drawn to the C.S.C. prison industry, known as CORCAN (derived from Corrections Canada). The revenue generated through the sale of CORCAN manufactured goods amounted to $10,308,000 during 1982-83, a 38% increase over 1981-82; and the value of agricultural products produced during 1982-83 was $1,280,000, an increase of 28.5% over 1981-82. The Correctional Service of Canada is restricted to selling goods and services to federal, provincial and municipal governments, and to charitable, religious and non-profit organisations unless special authorisation is obtained from the Treasury Board (Solicitor-General's Annual Report, 1982-83).

From a strictly economic viewpoint, prisoners can be viewed as 'liabilities' at no small cost to the public — $50,000 per year for each male prisoner and $62,000 for each female prisoner in maximum security. But when considered 'assets', this 'merchandise' generates hundreds of contracts, thousands of jobs, and millions of dollars in profits — profits which are not realised by the taxpayer but instead remain with CORCAN, the prison industry.

There is a parallel in the inherent contradictions in the management of prisons and the management of the international economy, where even less logic exists. For example, wealthy donor countries offering 'foreign aid' to poorer nations dare not embark on a genuine programme which would provide the recipients the means to develop their own resources, since it would eventually lead to the latter's need to also enter the international world export market. This would place it in the role of competing with the donor country, whose profit margin would thus be threatened, particularly from the delivery of its own services and sales which usually comprise eighty per cent of the tied aid bilateral agreement.

On the other hand, when the wealthy nation continues to extract the natural resources and exploit the cheap labour, the recipients are destined to impoverishment, including colossal debts. Sometimes this impoverishment reaches such a magnitude as to no longer remain hidden from the international media and becomes an international crisis, as in the 1984 African emergency. The disaster then requires outright charitable donations of food and funding.

A vicious circle.

The Criminal Justice System can hardly be expected to be more manageable, with its judiciary bogged down in courts of law, requiring more Remand Centres to hold more people, accused of breaking more laws, for longer periods of time even before they come to trial. The increased rate at which this growing number of people are being sentenced accelerates the need for constructing more and larger prisons at a colossal cost to already overburdened taxpayers.

Another vicious circle.

Depletion of human and natural resources whether through wars, greed or a prison system, needs to be halted before it destroys all in its path. The frightening link between militarism and the penal system is most competently demonstrated in an article by Helen Durie, an Ottawa criminologist, feminist, and anti-militarist activist:

> Just as nuclear weapons are used by the nuclear powers as the ultimate form of intimidation over those States which threaten their controlling interest over the world's resources and power, prisons similarly serve to maintain existing power and class relationships within every so-called developed society.
>
> While the State's military forces prepare for organised and legalised violence on an international scale, prisons (along with the police) are the State's internal arm of systematic legalised violence. Their very presence and

potential use is intimidating, and it doesn't require much analysis to see just who the reality, or the threat of imprisonment, is intended for.

It is important from the outset to make some distinction between the State's prison system, or police or military forces, and the individuals who serve in them, in describing them as purposeful violent institutions. It is probably fair to say that most men (and women, too, in this age of 'equal rights') who are recruited into one of these services are not doing so in order to be able to kill, or even to use violence.

They are enticed by the financial benefits and promise of variety, adventure and education opportunities, and by the culturally encouraged image of 'serving one's country.' That is how the State wants and needs it to be. It is not coincidental, either, of course, that those who do the front-line work — the real dirty work — in these professions are recruited predominantly from the lower socio-economic groups, where the lack of other educational, work and income opportunities make these enticements most salient and attractive. The fact that these people will be used by the State to carry out its wars against members of their own social groups at home and abroad is not part of their consciousness or service training.... While there are many differences between military training and the training received by police and prison guards, there are also many similarities (such as regular inter-force shooting competitions), because all services must learn to automatically resort to violence under certain conditions.

Today we are witnessing a simultaneous build-up of military capability and threats, along with an expansion of the tools and use of internal repression. This is a result of the increasing material gap between the haves and have-nots, within societies and on an international level, even while the foundations of capitalism are disintegrating in the face of growing competition for depleting resources and cheap labour, and increasing international political consciousness...

It is not surprising, then, in this climate of increasing social unrest, that prisons are being used more, new prisons are being built, and the violent and repressive measures that operate inside prisons are being extended. In Canada, a few examples are the construction of additional Special Handling Units (super-maximum segregation), installation of more and more draconian security equipment, searching and electronic surveillance of visitors, and increased power of the Parole Board to indefinitely delay (justifiable) release. The rising suicide rate in prisons is just one attestation to the increasing physical and psychological brutality (and futility) of imprisonment.

In Canada, there are close to 250 'correctional facilities' with over 25,000 prisoners on any given day, at an annual cost of more than $1 billion, increasing every year...

*And who are these prisons for?*

They are for those who learn only too well the meaning and power of 'success' in this society, and who dare to use the same tactics of intimidation, violence and lack of concern for others to achieve it as do the political and economic élite, but are without access to their legalised means... for those who can't afford the cost of legal protection... for those who dare to be poor and who refuse to live gratefully and passively on meagre handouts... for those who are born into a social-economic position which deprives them of the education and skills necessary to earn an 'honest' living and who dare to use other means to seek escape from their demeaning poverty... for Native people, whose dignified way of life has been stripped away by the white man and replaced with the dehumanising and deadly life of alcohol... for women who refuse any longer to be subjected to routine beatings from a man and who dare to fight back... for women whose socialised and economic dependency on men, and their fear of them, draws them into criminal complicity... for those who, without the cover of domestic or legal protection, dare to act out the sexual violence towards women and children that is glorified in our culture every day... for those who refuse to learn to kill and be the cannon fodder for wars that are fought to protect the interests of the political and economic élite... for those whose political awareness dares them to challenge and defy the political and economic structures that provide the basis for nuclear weapons and all of the other essential, immoral and oppressive elements of militarism...

For the State, the connections (between militarism and prison) come easily, as can be seen, for example, in the frequent conversion of decommissioned military bases to prisons, or the regularly touted proposal to sentence youthful offenders to a term in the military.

Activists need also to be aware of how easily and readily prisons are used to suppress dissent and, in this increasingly ominous climate of interconnectedness, recognise how integral a part of our political analysis the function of prisons must become. (*1984 And After*, 1984)

The Canadian Parliament in 1981 passed an Order-in-Council, called the Emergency Power Order (E.P.O.), which granted special powers to government ministries. A state of emergency would be declared when the nation was faced with natural disaster such as floods, earthquakes, etc., or a war, or breakdown of law and order. This non-debatable order (1981-1305) empowered the Solicitor-General's department, which includes the Correctional Service of Canada, the R.C.M.P., and the National Parole Board, among other responsibilities: "(No. 6) to establish, administer and operate civilian internment camps; and (No. 7) to facilitate the selective reduction and transfer of prison populations for the establishment of civilian internment camps." (Hansard, November 17, 1981)

The Prisoners' Rights Group (P.R.G.) requested a precise explanation of this little-publicised conundrum, and elicited the following reply in a letter dated May 10, 1982:

> No subsequent document has been issued that negates Numbers 6 and 7 of the Order; with further reference to Number 6, since PC 1981-1305 is a planning order only it provides no implementation authority. This means that no facilities may be constructed in advance of an actual war. I would like also to note that so far, this matter has a low priority and I have not yet seen any option from my officials and none are yet in preparation.

This non-explanation confirmed our worst fears — that this measure was primarily aimed at striking a balance between the government's version of the rights of the individual, and national security. Since pertinent details were conspicuously absent from the reply, we went on to request specific definitions of the following: 'to facilitate' — by what means?; 'selective' — by what criteria?; 'reduction' — meaning *what*?; 'transfer of prison populations' — from where to where?; and, 'to provide for the establishment of civilian internment camps' — what is the connection between the present prison population and civilian internment camps?

There has been no reply.

By the spring of 1983, another piece of legislation, Bill C-157, was introduced mainly to establish the Canadian Security Intelligence Service (C.S.I.S.), which was to be a replacement for R.C.M.P. agents who had been receiving bad press for their illegal acts. The C.S.I.S. Act would eliminate such embarrassments since it would permit security operatives to break the law when "it is reasonably necessary to enable them to perform."

Bill C-157 was strongly attacked by Alan Borovoy, legal counsel for the Canadian Civil Liberties Association (C.C.L.A.), as a mechanism whereby:

> ...citizens may have their conversation bugged, mail opened, homes searched and tax files invaded... a mandate to use such intrusive surveillance for the monitoring of 'activities'... in support of... acts of violence... for the purpose of achieving a political objective within Canada or a foreign state... this Bill must be seen as a threat to law-abiding people and legitimate dissent. (*Globe & Mail*, May 26, 1983)

With a few minor amendments, it was later passed as Bill C-9. A submission to the Standing Committee on Justice and Legal Affairs by the Vancouver Coalition against the C.S.I.S. summarised its objections on the grounds that the "mandate is too wide; the powers too broad; the accountability to the public and parliament too weak." It also concerned itself with the violation of the Charter of Rights and Freedoms in the clauses:

> 7.  Everyone has the right to life, liberty and security of person and the right not to be deprived thereof except

> in accordance with the principles of fundamental justice.
> 8. Everyone has the right to be secure against unreasonable search and seizures.

The submission expressed its belief that

> It is a dangerous law... threatens the rights and freedom of all Canadians in the name of an ill-defined and ambiguous 'national security'... accountability to Parliament would be minimal... the parliamentary mindset that views [former] Solicitor-General Warren Allmand as a 'communist' and to be put under surveillance, will not shift with an overnight change from uniform [R.C.M.P.] to civilian clothes.

With additional insight, it concludes: "This security debate is not happening in a vacuum... we cannot afford to experiment with the lives and freedoms of Canadians."

Perhaps as a way to assuage those who objected to the C.S.I.S., in November of 1984 the federal government appointed still another group to monitor the activities of the C.S.I.S. (*The Province*, Vancouver, November 30, 1984).

The C.S.I.S. enables the government to go beyond the rule of law with little accountability, a mandate which the Correctional Service of Canada utilises as a matter of routine — mail openings and censorship, physical and electronic surveillance, search of homes (cells), removal and destruction of personal effects, conversations tapped officially and unofficially — all of these have long been a familiar pattern in prisons in Canada. These repressive measures are carried out under the guise of 'institutional security', whereas in the public at large, they are carried out in the name of 'national security.'

The C.S.C. 'awards' prisoners Administrative Dissociation (time in 'the hole') for "suspicion of, or conspiracy to... upset the good order and discipline of the institution." It also cancels visiting rights on the pretext that "it is not considered necessary or desirable for... the security of the institution." What assurance do we have that the C.S.I.S. will not adopt similar attitudes towards those outside of prisons — with similar absence of accountability? What grounds are there to expect any different posture from the same government officials when they are confronted by protesters against that most deadly of all nuclear weapons, the Cruise missile, or by Native Indians exercising their Aboriginal rights?

Like the incarcerated who represent the most vulnerable layer of society in terms of inability to defend themselves against all manner of ill-treatment, we all face the risk of one day finding that the same methods may be employed against ordinary citizens. With the prisons having been used as a testing ground, the speed at which state and police control are being carried over into the rest of society gives cause for alarm.

Just as Correctional Service of Canada officials have the power to make arbitrary judgements about what may be perceived to be a threat to the security of the institution, and thus justify the use of repressive and violent measures, so the federal government can and has used arbitrary judgements as to what may constitute a threat to the security of the nation. An example is the Québec 1970 furore during the 'apprehended insurrection.' When the interpretation of 'national security' means retaining the *status quo*, then any group or individual who opposes the inequalities found in the justice system, or discrimination against minority groups, or the nuclear arms race, or even the filling out of census forms, can be considered to be a threat to national security.

> One of the most classic examples of the need to... resist the evils of society, is recorded in history. Martin Neimöller, pastor and former leader of the German Evangelical Church, was a man of rare courage and moral principle. Although he had defied Adolf Hitler to his face, he confessed after the war that his opposition had been inadequate and too late. Often quoted is his famous realisation that having stood by while the Nazis liquidated communists and trade unionists, Jews and Catholics — remaining silent because he belonged to none of those groups — he then had no one left to rise in his defence when his time came to be taken away... His resistance was fearless and uncompromising. [However] his greatest act of moral courage was his unflinching acceptance, after the war, of the responsibility he and many of his fellow countrymen

bore for the unspeakable suffering Hitlerism had inflicted
on mankind... (Gabor Mate, *Vancouver Sun*, March 2, 1984)

The article concludes with a message that must find its roots
in modern-day struggles, including the abolition of prisons:

> ...now, looking back, Neimöller was man enough to draw
> the only possible conclusion: *freedom is not divisible, it dis-*
> *appears from a society as soon as it is denied to any member of*
> *that society.* (Emphasis added)

## Capital Punishment

> Having a hangman won't solve unemployment or inflation,
> neither will it diminish the toll of violent crime. Over-
> whelming weight of evidence is that violent crime is most
> common in those societies where the state sets the example
> by putting the hand of every citizen on the rope. (Editorial,
> *Globe & Mail*)

As those concerned with civil liberties address themselves
to the threat of re-introduction of capital punishment, the
polarisation remains unyielding in many quarters. According
to recent polls, approximately seventy per cent of the Canadian
public are in favour of the death penalty, with many variations
as to its application. On the other side, those opposing the
death penalty continually produce convincing evidence and
arguments against it (see Appendix II).

Statistically, homicide records show that the death penalty
is not a deterrent. In 1975, the last year before abolition, the
murder rate was 3.09 per 100,000 of the population. After
capital punishment was struck from the criminal code in 1976,
the homicide rate fell to 2.74 per 100,000 by the end of 1983,
the last year records were available (Patrick Nagel, *Vancouver
Sun*, October 11, 1984).

In an attempt to focus on the various forms of murder and
to place it in a wider context, it is worth looking at other
relevant statistics, while keeping in mind that all unnatural

deaths are unnecessary. In 1981, of 100,000 construction workers, 191 died on the job in Canada; in the fishing undustry, 147 out of 100,000 died; and forestry workers' deaths tolled 91 (Labour Canada). The burden of guilt in these deaths lies, for the most part, with the employer, who invariably puts profits before human life. But these are called accidental and are considered one of the risks one has to take on entering the specific industry.

In the case of the police force, on-the-job deaths totalled 83 in the 23 years since Statistics Canada began keeping records — approximately 3½ deaths per year. These deaths, however, are not considered occupational hazards, but are seen as horrifying crimes, an affront to us all, which must be avenged. While there is little public outcry about the deaths or injuries of most workers, a high degree of emotionalism surrounds the death or injury of a police officer.

While the chance of a police officer being killed on duty is about six times greater than the risk faced by most civilians, it is far less than that of a miner, construction worker, transportation or public utility worker. The chances of anyone dying on the job are twenty times greater than those of being murdered. Another consideration, without putting the onus on any one person, is the responsibility for other stress and poverty-related deaths such as those brought on by heart attacks, malnutrition, tuberculosis and alcoholism.

Those people in favour of 'bringing back the noose' argue with more zeal than logic, which is understandable in a society which purportedly espouses the philosophy that life is precious. Their arguments include the Biblical 'eye for an eye' pronouncement; that an executed murderer cannot kill again; that those guilty of vicious murders do not deserve to live; that the alternative of life imprisonment places an unnecessary financial drain on the community; and that the murder of police and prison guards, in their role as public servants, must be avenged. Implicit in these viewpoints is that the restoration of the death penalty will automatically lead to the deterrence of killings, and as such, warrants strong support. The possibility of an error in judgement which would lead to the irrevocable execution of an innocent person appears to be of little, if any, import to those in favour of capital punishment.

According to Robert Martin, an Ontario law professor: "By demanding that the advocates of capital punishment provide reasoned arguments to support their positions we expose the barrenness of their position, and we may perhaps ensure that we remain a country which does not seek to maintain public order by stooping to the level of the murderer" (*Globe & Mail*, October 11, 1984).

If we base ourselves on the consensus that *all* life is precious and *every* avoidable death is a tragedy, then we must give credence to arguments against the death penalty.

"It would seem not to be the mark of a civilised society for no other reason than vengeance, to kill people who have done dastardly things. There is a grave risk in showing the populace we don't put a great deal of stock in people's lives..." is the opinion of Reg Robson, past president of the B.C. Civil Liberties Association (*Vancouver Sun*, September 29, 1984). And an editorial in *Macleans* (October 8, 1984) tells us that "There is no clear evidence that murder by the state serves as a deterrent to the horror of murder by individuals and if simple state-sanctioned revenge is the main driving force behind the new campaign... then logic no longer plays a part in the debate... At the same time, capital punishment tends to be a relatively facile concept for many people to support because those who would suffer the ultimate penalty tend to be social rejects, underprivileged and unattractive, a minority by definition..."

Since the issue of capital punishment is an emotion-packed one, it is essential to approach it in a reasonable manner. Addressing ourselves to both logic and emotion, I would advance two more reasons to retain the present law — one pertaining to the net-widening factor, the other to public fear.

The net-widening factor begins with the public's desire to restore the death penalty because of this season's understandable revulsion toward the 'Clifford Olsons' (mass child rapist-murderers) in our society, as well as the increasing number of duty-police deaths. However, with such a law in place, there is nothing to prevent this government or any future government from passing amendments to include others. First, the law might include those who kill in 'crimes of passion,' where there never was any intent and the killer is extremely remorseful;

or, it might include those prisoners labelled by prejudiced prison staff as 'dangerous offenders' who are considered not only a threat to society, but also to the institution in which they are imprisoned.

From there, it would be a simple matter to extend the net with one small amendment to include those who threaten 'national security.' In which case, who is to say that concerned citizens exercising their democratic right to commit non-violent acts of civil disobedience as they protest the testing of that deadliest of all projectiles, the Cruise missile, or the Trident submarine passing through west coast waters, would not be considered a threat to national security, labelled 'terrorists' and 'traitors' and sentenced to death? The mechanism is already in place to intern civilians who may be considered a threat to national security. Restoration of the death penalty might be seen as another step towards eliminating civilians engaged in legitimate protest against the state. In this Star Wars decade, with both defence and prison industry budgets on the increase, the lawmakers-war-profiteers might well consider such people a terrible threat.

The second reason offered for retaining the present laws pertaining to capital punishment concerns public fear and insecurity. We live in a time of severe economic depression, when many of the material goods we once took for granted are gradually slipping away from us, our rights on the job and in society are being eroded, and the values we once held dear are apparently disappearing. While politicians, lawmakers and economists do little to improve the situation, in our powerlessness we cry out for some assurance that the fears and instability we are suffering will be removed. Lacking the correct solutions to the economic, political and social causes of our insecurities, and looking for someone to blame and a way to calm our fears, we clamour for the blood of the most vulnerable scapegoat — the convicted murderer.

Those in power do little to stem the controversy over capital punishment, for many reasons. One is that while people are occupied in debate over the right to legally murder another human being, they are not addressing themselves to, or disrupting the government with, such fundamental issues as militarism, poverty, or the increase in state control in all areas of society.

Professor Irwin Waller considered "capital punishment... a reaction to murder and not a way of trying to save human lives," and felt that we would be "spending our time a lot better trying to find ways of saving lives, of reducing the murder rate [by] gun control laws [and] more reasonable divorce laws; and other measures focussing on family violence would see reductions by fifty to a hundred murders in a year" (CBO Radio, September 4, 1984). The argument, then, is that we should be concerning ourselves not only with saving lives on a large scale, but also with improving the quality of life for the 'rejects, underprivileged, and unattractive' of our society.

Should a free vote be called in Canadian Parliament to deal with the existing law, which banished the death penalty in 1976, we can take heart from the last such vote taken in the British Parliament in July 1983. The polls there also showed that British public opinion strongly favoured restoration and Prime Minister Margaret Thatcher herself voted for capital punishment. The vote was 368 to 223 *against* restoration of the death penalty (*Macleans*, October 8, 1984).

The Canadian Catholic Conference Task Force for the Continued Abolition of the Death Penalty (1972) provided the following food for thought: "The question of the death penalty... ought to focus *not* on whether a convicted murderer 'deserves to die'... The focus should be on us: would Canadians as a community try to break the escalating spiral of violence by refraining from violence as a deterrent?"

> Ultimately, we are forced to face that gut-level question that contributes to the highly emotional nature of most discussions of capital punishment. Is the murderer human or has he resigned from the human race and thus deserving of no human consideration? To answer this question, we have to face, without flinching, the grim realities of all that is involved in the death penalty; to recognise that it is not merely the criminal we are considering, it is all those others, and finally, ourselves.

And until we face the harsh facts of what happens on death row and in the execution room, in the witness room, and in the offices and homes of prison officials, lawyers and judges, we are not entitled to have an opinion and call it reasonable and just. (Colin Turnbull, *Death by Decree*, undated)

# Chapter 4

# Beyond Prisons: Where Do We Go From Here?

*Instead of dreaming with our eyes open, we should be practical and concrete, setting for ourselves only those goals that we can actually attain, and concentrating on the best means of attaining them.*

Antonio Gramsci

# 4     Beyond Prisons: Where Do We Go From Here?

*The prison at present is at best a monumental evil and a burning shame to society. It ought not merely to be reformed but abolished as an institution for the punishment and degradation of human beings.*

Eugene Debs

Two roads face us as we search for the most expedient solution to the present chaos in the prison system: accept the trend towards more control, which historically begins with one of the most vulnerable groups — prisoners; *or*, proceed to dismantle the billion-dollar Criminal Justice System with all its vested political and economic interests.

In my view, there is only one choice — dismantle the system. The first step would then be to release to the community the approximately eighty per cent of the 26,000 incarcerated in Canada on any given day who were not convicted for violent crime and are not considered dangerous, so that they can work and make restitution to their victims and support themselves and their families. Following that, the next fifteen per cent who are not quite ready to return to work should be provided with the appropriate medical, economic, and social care required to raise them to the level of the first category. For the remaining five per cent who may have been judged to require further detention, only one prison would be needed, with a humane and creative environment which would remove the degrading effects on both the keeper and the kept.

However, in a country where close to two million are unemployed, and considering the stigma of being an ex-convict, the possibility of finding employment for the numbers mentioned is greatly reduced. In light of this, the question must be faced — are too many people being held in prison for too long because of tough economic times, and if so, is it practical to house this surplus of 'hostages to the economy' in prisons? Is a radical transformation of current values required?

145

Following this line of thought, while many would support prison reform, particularly in areas such as medical care, visiting rights, etc., do we really mean to perpetuate the prison system itself, indefinitely? When we call for alternatives such as half-way houses, community services, and fines, are we accepting more of the same but with minor modifications so that prison will be a little less cruel and a little more humane?

And when we finally reach the pinnacle of a call for abolition, do we mean: more sophisticated methods to 'incapacitate without incarceration'; or do we mean: *no more prisons*?

Alternatives which extend the Criminal Justice System's range of control — net-widening, in the new terminology — operate through channels such as probation, parole, community services, family courts, treatment centres — even the possibility of penal colonies. More insidious alternatives, under the guise of abolition, are surveillance schemes such as house arrest, or employing electronic bracelet attachments or implants under the skin to signal the wearer's movements, which can be expected to follow the earlier lobotomy procedures — only a step removed from the ghastly, mind-destroying Electro-Convulsive Therapy (shock treatments).

Aiming at short-term prisons as a last resort for the smallest number of people for the shortest period of time, the following 'crimes' must first be banished: the death penalty, Special Handling Units, solitary confinement, excessive sentences, forced involuntary transfers, and physical and psychological abuse.

Directing efforts on behalf of those who are the main victims of economic and social deprivation as well as those of racial and sexist discrimination, would effectively demystify the predicament of prisoners. It would also more accurately individualise assistance so that every accused whose conviction has been successfully appealed would represent a victory for de-carceration, which means *keeping them out of prison*. All prisoners who win a speedy parole release as soon as they are eligible or have their unreal sentence computations corrected in their favour would represent a victory for excarceration — *getting them out of prison*.

Usually, exposés of the 'shocking reality of life behind bars' manage only to astound, agitate and infuriate. They appeal

146

mainly to the emotions. Seldom do they draw political conclusions by examining the prison system as a function of the state — an instrument for class, racial and national oppression. Publication of prisoners' autobiographies and other harrowing descriptions of prison life by reformists are not a threat to the establishment insofar as they merely describe what exists; and by now, we *know* what exists. What *is* a threat is any truly political analysis which proves that prison conditions are not unique, positioned as they are in the increasingly controlled society in which we live.

Taking into account the 'legal' violence applied to prisoners, it is important to recognise how its recurrence is generated, which is then used to create the image of the 'dangerous person' who must be caged for the protection of society. But it is really society which is 'dangerous'. Latin American bishops, meeting at Medellin, avoided "...comparing or identifying the unjust violence of the oppressors, who support this 'iniquitous system,' with the just violence of the oppressed, who are forced into the position of having to use violence if they are to gain their freedom."*

Society is based upon an unequal distribution of power and opportunity, disguising its discrimination against the poor and the powerless. It uses prisons as an instrument to create a criminal milieu that the ruling class can control. The existence of a just system of criminal justice in an unjust society remains a contradiction in terms, since no society can call itself civilised as long as one section has the power to brutalise another. Eventually this perversity infects the whole of society and turns it back upon itself. We need only consider the madness of the arms race.

The prison as we now know it has been described as a product of the Industrial Revolution, which created a need for cheap labour and which used the captive criminal to its own advantage. Even the legitimacy of slavery was not seriously questioned until the late eighteenth century. As modern states were drawn into imperial wars, more repression was required to control the ensuing economic and political chaos.

---

* The General Conference of the Latin American hierarchy adopted by 920 priests (*The Rebel Church in South America*, 1974).

The use of prisons as a means of ensuring social control is fundamental to all societies. Outrages practised against prisoners which some find so appalling should not be so difficult to comprehend, as they are consistent with prison structures which governments use to retain power. Those who are labelled a 'threat to society' become the incarcerated symbols used to strengthen the state's authority.

> In prison we are governed and controlled by the same attitudes that govern and control the lives of people outside the prisons. The attitudes are [just] more to the extreme... we are forced into resisting force. (John Clutchette, a Soledad Brother quoted in *If They Come in the Morning*, 1971)

Penal institutions are a microcosm of the violent world which generates them. Attempts to separate the violence of the prison system from this reality is a political naiveté which Canadians can ill-afford.

When the illegal activities of the R.C.M.P. during the 1970 F.L.Q. episode in Québec came to light, editorials astutely directed attention to the repressive direction which the government was taking. Like any other twentieth century nation, in order to maintain its power, it has to control the military, the police and the prison system. Any person or group daring to criticise and expose these functions has to expect, and will receive, the full brunt of authoritarian vengeance. Only informed and determined support of civil and human rights — particularly of prisoners who are supposed to be deprived only of their 'freedom of movement' (that is, rendered geographically immobile) — can redirect this system's values.

Why do we tolerate prisons? A carefully prepared report on Crime and Punishment in America offers one answer:

> If social factors cannot be controlled or predicted, the relevance of individualised treatment is decreased and may be negligible... A prisoner detained to prevent crimes that could be avoided by social reforms may bear a greater resemblance to a scapegoat than to either a patient or a public enemy... To date our society has largely ignored this dilemma. (*Struggle for Justice*, 1971)

Despite official studies such as that by the Solicitor-General (Annual Report 1982-83) which indulge in make-believe plans to "...define optional ways of meeting the challenge of maintaining a humanitarian discretionary system that is just and equitable to inmates and society as a whole," there is really no lack of knowledge of the actual state of affairs in Canadian prisons, nor is there any need for further investigation into its 'problems'.

With all the resources at its disposal, the Criminal Justice System fails to take advantage of scientific findings to unriddle specific disorders. For example: instead of still another experiment with sex offenders, this time in laboratories to measure genital response as the sex offenders react to video shows of child pornography, we could surely profit from studies such as reported in "The Chemistry of Violence" (*Queen's Quarterly*, Spring 1984) which apparently found that a very simple hair analysis is sufficient

> ...to test violent males to determine whether their nutrient levels suggest selective retention or mal-absorption of certain elements... where psychiatry and counselling have proven largely ineffective in readjusting violent personalities and integrating them back into society.

Another approach is that of the Prison Research Education Action Project (P.R.E.A.P.) in an article in *Strategies for the 80s*, which includes programmes for those sexually violent people who *do* require temporary separation from society. Places of restraint are needed while re-education and retraining take place, and P.R.E.A.P. is clear that no one should ever be excluded from humane conditions or the opportunity for changing violent, physically harmful behaviour.

This is not to suggest that every prisoner will be 'cured' by any of the above methods. However, there are remedies, some yet to be explored, that could take the place of speculative ventures which tend to distort rather than heal.

Another factor to consider in decreasing the prison population concerns the black market in drugs, particularly heroin. Political intrigues surrounding heroin must be unmasked, too. For example — the Pentagon's utilisation of the illicit international drug trade as a means of intervention in its client states, much as it used the 'Foreign Aid programmes' in the last decade, and the adaptation of the Food as Weapons schemes in the present decade.

The Canadian Medical Association (C.M.A.) has already endorsed the medical use of heroin, calling the country's 18,000 heroin addicts not criminals, but victims of thirty years of misguided political and police prosecution. According to Dr. Bill Ghent, chairman of the C.M.A. Health Care Council, a day's supply of 'legal' heroin costs only 20¢, compared to $100 a day for the impure variety sold on the street. "Heroin addiction is in truth a dependency syndrome such as diabetes, and it should not be considered a crime to be so affected..." he stated, claiming that heroin addiction "had been made a target of political and police powers that would do justice to Attila the Hun" (*Vancouver Sun*, August 22 and November 30, 1984). Were the drug trade fully exposed, it would deprive the Criminal Justice System of one of its main sources of 'merchandise'.

To curb further such excesses, both governments and prison bureaucracies should be subjected to relentless public exposure.

An element which is rarely, if ever, included in criminal studies is described by the Quaker Committee on Jails and Justice (Q.C.J.J.) in an undated brochure:

> Crime is no respecter of wealth, power or class; the prevalence of unprosecuted middle and upper-class violation is... a phenomenon... labelled white-collar crime. Unbiased statistics... would probably show that the proportion of criminals in various segments of a population increases with wealth and power... it seems certain that the loss caused to victims of such 'rich' crimes far exceeds that of the usual lower-class criminality.

Plainly, a community without any programmes in place into which embittered people are released must itself be guilty of imprudent planning. Or is this 'imprudence' in any way akin to the drastic cutbacks in employment which create vast pools of jobless that employers draw upon for cheap labour, which in turn weakens the organised labour movement? Social service cutbacks that result in more problems for the young, the elderly, the sick, the handicapped, the homeless and the jobless accelerate the perceived need for more prison construction as a means to cope with predictable insecurities.

When those individuals and corporations with the most wealth pay little or no taxes while the basic needs of others who are told to wait until the 'economy bounces back' are neglected, it must be apparent that the state is largely responsible and is hardly likely to make genuine attempts to solve the problem. At a time when the prison system is described by a Crown Prosecutor as "being out of control" (*Whig Standard*, January 31, 1984) it must also be viewed as a product of the same policy of calculated neglect, and not as some economic aberration.

But there is a silver lining. The Correctional Service of Canada continues to prosper through its CORCAN industries. In Bowden Medium Security Institution, Alberta, prisoners are employed in the production of "...furniture, upholstery, carpentry, metal products and the *Drone Rocket Project*... part of an innovative... modification of a number of discontinued American-made drone rockets to be used for target practice by the Canadian Navy..." (Emphasis added) (*Let's Talk*, March 15, 1984).

An interesting sidelight on this topic is found in an American assessment:

> A legislative committee reported in 1979 'as more prisoners are incarcerated, industry expands and more goods are produced but the costs of building prisons, administering prison programmes and guarding a captive labour force becomes more and more excessive.' (*A Road of Social and Economic Bankruptcy*, by Maygene Giari, forthcoming)

Prison activists are frequently asked why anyone would want to pour their energies into helping lawbreakers, who apparently showed no concern for their victims, yet now seek help to obtain their own rights. We could answer with: why not join forces against the warlords, and the polluters and destroyers of the planet? It is not merely a matter of helping individuals survive, although there is nothing wrong with broadening the horizons of humanitarianism. There should be no differentiation between striving for a better world for *all* and reacting to personal miseries around us. Rather, it is a matter of demystifying the widespread concept of prisoners as one homogeneous body. 'Groupism' is a formula which, like racism, disposes of an entire group, assuming that some are superior by nature to others. While the need to reject this judgemental error would seem self-evident, the constant reference to prisoners as a single group leads to some very bizarre attitudes.

It also plays into the hands of those whose vested interest is to perpetuate this image in order to maintain the high 'count'. How else can the stream of studies by the C.J.S. hierarchies about the 'need to reduce sentences,' 'to find alternatives to incarceration,' 'to consider prisons only as a last resort,' be reconciled to the unvarnished truth — the increasing size, number and restrictions of the prison scene.

Setting aside the type of crime for which the person was convicted, here is a lawbreaker — a man or woman — committed to the most lawless institution in the land... where health, fire and building inspections are not conducted by the municipality but by the institution itself, and where there is neither the rule of law nor access to reasonable attitudes on the part of the various officials upon whom those convicted must depend for all their basic needs.

It is a place where constant humiliation as well as physical beatings are so much a part of daily life as to be considered routine; where transcripts and grievances are 'lost'; incoming and outgoing mail is undelivered; where lawyers' calls are unreported; visitors are turned away for nonsensical reasons; families and assistants scheduled to attend N.P.B. hearings arrive only to be told that the hearing date had been changed to — invariably — a time *prior* to the scheduled date; where urgent medical attention is deferred; grievances are dealt with unsatisfactorily; personal effects are lost or damaged in transit from one region to another; where prisoners return after a cell search to find treasured photo albums and irreplaceable personal belongings ripped apart; are forbidden to appear personally to have witnesses at internal reviews which then accept verbatim charges from guards; are forbidden to examine personal files

152

to correct disparaging and inaccurate evidence; where strip-searches including body cavities are conducted even when confined to the hole 23½ hours per day, obviously with no possible outside contact; where involuntary transfers to other regions are enforced while preparing appeal and parole applications; planted drugs and 'shivs' are found in one's cell *after* search... the list is endless and lunatic.

Should the reader be inclined to brush all this aside as the ramblings of a 'bleeding heart,' go try and penetrate beyond the 'security' barriers which block one-to-one conversations, permitting only monitored talk either by telephone or by the latest devices now in place at every visiting table where Maximum Security prisoners meet with their families and friends. The first thing you will discover is that you can't find out. Without determined efforts to maintain contact when barred from visiting, or when lawyers assist, the above provocations would remain hidden.

Prisoners, subjected to the vengeful treatment described in Chapter 2, and who rebel against the unfairness of their circumstances, are further aggravated by their sense of powerlessness. Labelled 'criminals', they are not insensitive to the fact that they are despised and rejected. Surrounded with frustrations that drive their cell-mates to suicide and helpless to come to their aid, prisoners accumulate a cynical resistance to all authority. This manifests itself when they finally return to the 'civilised' society which, for the most part, ignores, in the words of Ramsey Clark:

> ... [the]dehumanizing effect on the individual of slums, racism, ignorance and violence... poverty and unemployment and idleness, of generations of malnutrition... prenatal neglect, of sickness and disease... dirty, ugly, unsafe, overcrowded housing, of alcohol and narcotic addiction... [these are] the fountainheads of crime. (*Crime in America*, 1970)

When perception and understanding are discarded, common sense dictates that victims rebel and their allies become strident. The struggle to abolish the prison system must be included in every outcry against those who monopolise control. Failure to make this link seriously undermines any political analyses of war, racism, poverty, and other forms of injustice.

The view of those who would minimise the role of the prison system stems, in part, from the attitude that prisons are filled with the dregs of society and as such merit no concern. In reality, since we are dealing with the most political of social institutions, it is for *political* reasons that we should be paying more attention to the corruption and stupidity of one of Canada's major growth industries — the prison system. The turmoil of our penitentiary system exists within, and is related to, the larger social context of world disorder.

The pattern of institutionalised violence has become so commonplace that most prison activists and lawyers have reluctantly come to accept its seeming inevitability. They feel helpless to change it. However, we can no longer afford to accept that the society which repudiates violence in its streets, at the same time condones violence against those unfortunates held in custody. No longer limited to prisoners, the toll of victims is widening — in the form of police beatings, car chases, and unwarranted shoot-outs. If this wall of impotence is to be breached, it is essential to understand that the prison system is also an integral part of the drift towards the authoritarianism of our alleged liberal democracy.

This means not only redefining policies, but also recognising the need to seek support that can effectively meet this crisis. It is within this context that prison activists must strive to build bridges with other groups. This is now beginning to happen. A similar message was offered at the 1982 Congress of Corrections in Ontario by William Kunstler, the prominent American civil rights lawyer:

> I have been led to believe... that there are human answers for human problems and that there is an obligation upon all of us to seek those answers in an intelligent and determined way. Reason, Descartes tells us, is the highest attribute of humankind, the quality that supposedly sets us apart from other animals... the creation of such an outlaw prison class will, in the long run, jeopardise and perhaps destroy the freedom of us all as well as advance the dehumanisation process that constantly gnaws at the

fabric of our vaunted civilisation. (*Jericho: Newsletter of the National Moratorium on Prison Construction*, Winter 1982)

In the ongoing search for ways to tackle the problem, traditional prison reformists, despite their unquestionable sincerity and motivation, can be deluded into thinking that painstaking efforts will fundamentally change the prisoners' lot — that at long last brutalities will end, and the prison will become a reasonably respectable segment of a reasonably respectable society, regardless of its irregularities.

But that is not how prisoners view it: "When pressures for reform lead to demands to relieve 'overcrowding' by adding new cells or bed space the result is inevitable: the coercive net of the justice system will be spread over a larger number of people, entrapping them for longer periods of time " (*Struggle for Justice*, 1971). And as Jessica Mitford writes in *Kind and Usual Punishment*:

> It becomes imperative to distinguish between two types of reform proposals: those which will result in strengthening the prison bureaucracy, designed to perpetuate and reinforce the system, and those which to one degree or another challenge the whole premise of prison and move in the direction of eventual abolition.

How should one interpret the rare outspokenness of the C.S.C. Commissioner, Donald R. Yeomans, when he "looks at ways to reduce our prison population"? Or when he expounds with unusual candour on how "...criminological studies indicate that long sentences are no more effective in reducing crime than short sentences... From a cost perspective, it makes no sense to impose a long prison sentence where a short one would do... A Canadian study shows reconviction rates are higher among unemployed as opposed to employed offenders released on parole... Since unemployment or under-employment is a contributing factor in recidivism, society should examine the role it can play in providing employment for ex-inmates and training opportunities for inmates.... The unemployment rate among fifteen to twenty-four-year-olds is three times what it was fifteen years ago... Unless we do something to integrate

155

more of those youths in the world of work [we should] not be surprised to see a large proportion of them in our prisons in the years to come."*

One would have to match these comments to the actions which distinguish this particular jurisdiction. The cold, hard facts, as listed in *Prisoners of Isolation*, are that "...by the year 2001 there will be 789 serving 25-year sentences for first-degree murder. [All being minimum sentences *before parole eligibility*, which can mean that they will *never* get out.] As of March 1983 there were 595 serving life sentences with minimum parole eligibility of ten years or more, and 185 doing 25-year minimum."

Even with the awareness and knowledge displayed above, we see that the good Commissioner and his colleagues have accomplished little in the way of producing positive results, since there is a growing number of prisoners serving longer periods under more brutal conditions. The old cry that the custodians cannot be held responsible for the people that are sent to them by the judiciary is no longer acceptable as long as they remain silent while prisoners continue to be beaten and shot at, and their suicide rate mounts.

> The struggle to end oppression in prisons is only a battle in a much larger war. That war is one to change an economic system that dictates that prisons be built and that they be oppressive to those who are labelled 'undesirable'. Our prison systems will only change when we are finally successful in changing the basic values of this society — when people will come before the dollar. (*Newsletter*, Prisoners' Rights Coalition of Santa Fe, March 1984)

A brief examination of the Dutch Criminal Justice System will illustrate how incongruous is any comparison between its philosophy of reform (albeit in an entirely different historical setting) and the reality of its North American counterpart.

---

* Donald R. Yeomans, to the Institute on Donations and Public Affairs Research, Toronto, October 24, 1979.

The following information is from a paper by C. Kelk in *Contemporary Crisis 7* entitled "The Humanity of the Dutch Prison System and the Prisoners' Consciousness of Their Legal Rights."

During the Second World War various social classes came into contact with the inside of prisons as a result of acts of resistance against the occupying German army. This led as early as 1947 to the initiation of a general reform of the Dutch prison system, which had not significantly increased in size in 140 years, although the population of the country had increased fourfold.

Each institution was to have a Supervisory Board consisting of independent citizens. It was intended that these Boards, by exercising regular control and supervision, would create a balance for the extensive prerogatives and power which were at the same time accorded to the Director. That is, the Board would guard against the abuse of power, and arbitrariness.

In 1958 a collection of prisoners' letters was published, based on a belief in their human dignity and the importance of continued trust as responsible persons, which called attention to their position as legal subjects despite their crimes. A storm of public indignation resulted. Functionaries were, for the first time, confronted with the implications of their own actions. What had been achieved, in any case, was the first piercing of the hermetically closed prison situation. Prisoners' voices could now be heard from captivity.

Resocialising measures were sought in the improvement of material as well as personal conditions. Radical reductions in the number of detentions imposed by judicial authorities were sought, based on the view that prisons are the expression of a situation of genuine social inequality, and that prison sentences are seriously damaging for the individual.

The Coornhert League (similar in some ways to the Howard League for Penal Reform in England, a visiting organisation with a measure of input into Administration decisions) had two perspectives: the fundamentally abolitionist, *and* that which aimed at improvement of concrete situations.

There were similar developments in England, with Preservation of the Rights of Prisoners (P.R.O.P.) in 1972, and in Norway, with the Association for Penal Reform (K.R.O.M.) in 1967. According to a K.R.O.M. study, "differences of opinion developed with both, sharply divided between 'escalating revolts and strikes' and that of offering no immediate concrete help." In Norway, the association subsequently chose a 'politics of abolition,' which included working toward the abolition of juvenile prisons, forced labour, and so on.

The paper concludes with: "All in all it is difficult to assess the concrete influences these movements have: a clearly repressive system is usually not open to outside interference, while in a more humane, less repressive system, there is often not much more to be done than achieving marginal improvements which eliminate the basis for more radical actions, which in turn has repercussions on the unity and solidarity of these movements." Obviously this is not the nature of the problem confronting North American prisoners.

In the U.S., Dr. Jerry Miller, during his appointment as Director of the Department of Youth Services in Massachusetts, managed in only three years to empty all but one juvenile prison by transferring the young prisoners into a variety of community alternative living situations. "Swift and massive change is the only sure way to phase out institutions.... Slow phased winding down can mean no winding down, and often ensures they'll wind up again..." (*Instead of Prisons*, 1976).

At present, Dr. Miller has turned his professional expertise to setting up five non-profit offices called the National Centre on Institutions and Alternatives, which specialises in pre- and post-release programming and personal assistance. This has proven to be a very effective way to simultaneously prove the worth of the abolition movement and provide successful working examples. In *USA Today* (September 21, 1983) Dr. Miller maintains that "The solution is not as elusive as those who run the system would have us believe. It's not so much a lack of resources as a lack of will. If there is anything the system doesn't need, it's more money to do more of the same... build more prisons."

To reassure those who may still feel apprehensive about abolishing prison systems, let us now move on to the call for abolition from other knowledgeable persons.

At a Symposium at the University of Victoria in 1979 called The Future of Prisons, Professor J. H. Mohr, a member of the

Law Reform Commission, had this to say in "Imprisonment — A Policy Without Direction":

> We have lived for about 200 years with the embarrassment of prisons, and I call it an embarrassment because it must be obvious to us now that we have used one rationalisation after another and that we have used up all the rationalisations since we are back to the utilitarian beginnings, if I read the present mood correctly. We must be wary by now of our own good intentions to get a deeply flawed system off the hook.

Michael Kroll, a former editor of *Jericho*, writes:

> We throw people in prison whose crimes against property could better be addressed through restitution [to victims] and community services. We could rely on supervised probation if we poured the kind of money into that system that now goes down the prison sinkhole. But we are mired in the prison experiment, unable to free ourselves, unwilling to be bold and creative... we will pay a terrible price for our failure.

The dust jacket of the book *British Prisons* by Mike Fitzgerald and Joe Sim (1982) states:

> This book is an unapologetic attack upon every aspect of the British penal system and has no room at all for any reassuring talk about minor changes or gradual modifications which might get us over the present crisis...

At a Seminar on Penal Philosophies and Practices for the 70s, sponsored by the Australian Institute of Criminology and dominated by prison administrators with a sprinkling of academics, a remarkable resolution was adopted. Initiated by the Prisoners' Action Group (P.A.G.), it reads, in part:

> The Conference asserts that prisons are ultimately unnecessary... As a concrete expression of that goal, the Conference should assert... that prisons as penal sanction should disappear.

In our own society, short-term plans should be directed toward helping to keep prisoners alive and well by opening up the prisons to responsible monitoring, with accountability to the outside community.

A useful component in this battle would be to enlist meaningful media contact. I made an attempt to initiate regular monthly press conferences when I was a member of the Citizens' Advisory Committee at the B.C. Pen in 1976. Such a process would benefit the prison Administration, which could demonstrate its sincerity in making improvements; the prisoners would not feel pressured into hostage-taking in order to air their grievances and have them corrected; and the media itself could become a more creative, investigative force by researching a specific area each month — segregation, transfers, health care — rather than sensationalising crises, which only contributes to the public's misunderstandings. The authorities did not respond to the suggestion.

Conferences, symposia, commissions, hearings, inquiries — all take place regularly to deal with the 'incarcerated offenders' and what can be done for them, for the system, and for the bureaucracy which lives off them. There is a general consensus that the system is riddled with problems and that is the reason these sessions are held so frequently — to try to find the answers, plug the holes, and above all, to keep the system functional so the thousands of jobs do not disappear. After all, the prison empire must not be allowed to collapse upon itself.

Emmanuel Margolis, in the *Connecticut Bar Journal* (1972), put it this way:

> No objective examination of the best prison system can avoid the conclusion that it is primitive, coercive and dehumanizing. No rational, let alone scientific appraisal of treatment or rehabilitation programs within the prison setting, can assess them as anything but a total sham. The best efforts of correctional personnel are doomed to frustration and failure, whether measured by recidivism rates or any other reasonable standards of 'progress'.

Before proceeding to accounts of specific actions in this field, excerpts from a Simon Fraser University student's thesis are offered:

> Should prisons — as we now know and use them — continue to exist? Should prisons, in any shape or form, exist at all? The first raises the possibility of reform or change within the institution itself, the second quite obviously poses the more extreme challenge of abolition.

> The concept of punishment as an exercise of power — the bottom line is social control.

> Prisoners' rights [stress] two basic and complementary demands: 1) the rule of law to prevail inside prisons, and 2) creation of prisoner empowerment.

> Abolitionists should push for abolition on its own terms without becoming implicated in the system demand for a *quid pro quo* [equivalent] outcome.

> Condemning those who commit violence to suffer violence themselves can hardly be expected to reduce the total amount of violence we all experience.

> The 'you have to do something about crime' argument is disposed of on the grounds that 'you *don't* have to do something that demonstrably doesn't work.'

> [Society] merely focuses on crime as an individual problem and for the most part ignores the wider social, economic and political setting in which crime is located.

> Prisons do not exist in a vacuum; they are part of a political, social, economic and moral order.

> A serious attack on the 'crime problem' would probably involve, at a very minimum, efforts directed at reducing unemployment, barriers to teen-age entry into the job market, and other structural features of the labour market which impede the pursuit of lawful style of living in the community... unlikely as these changes may be, even they would probably be insufficient and we may well need 'an even broader attack on inequalities in both income and the ownership of productive property.'

*Why prisons at all? (The Existential Problem of Prisons: Reform or Abolition*, Mary Rose Binchy, 1983)

Complementing these views are those of Gerhard Mueller in his essay "Imprisonment and its Alternatives":

> For all practical purposes, imprisonment means the caging of human beings either singly or in pairs or groups.... If there were the slightest scientific proof that the placement of human beings into boxes or cages for any length of time, even overnight, had the slightest beneficial effect, perhaps such a system might be justifiable. There is no such proof; consequently, I should think that a massive attack on the constitutionality of the caging of human beings is in order. (*Instead of Prisons*, 1976)

Since there is a terrible need to combat the pattern of blatant disregard for maintaining even the appearance of truth which persists in most areas of prison life, and since attempts are being made to silence those who are still free to speak out, it becomes crucial that everything published or acted out on this issue should contribute to decisive analyses and plans for action. An unyielding solidarity with those already in prison is a good place to start. The treatment of prisoners in Canada is indeed 'cruel,' but it is not 'unusual'. Every punitive act tests not only the prisoner's capacity to survive, but our capacity to permit such suffering.

The first essential remains to create a prison system scrupulously accountable to the community, and to avoid becoming enmeshed in the bureaucratic web. Following this, thought has been given to a Community Prison Board (C.P.B.) similar in purpose to Hospital, Education, and Parks Boards. The C.P.B. would thus include — in addition to those directly involved in the operation of prisons and other detention centres — friends and families of prisoners, ex-prisoners, agencies such as the Elizabeth Fry and John Howard Societies, prisoners' rights groups, health care centres, women and children abuse centres, representatives from associations for the mentally, physically, and learning disabled, as well as from Native Indian groups and ethnic minorities. The C.P.B. would thus include representatives from all elements of a community, the same community from which prison populations are drawn.

In addition to its educational and preventative value, the C.P.B. would also arrange to install a Prisoner Liaison (P.L.) in each prison to maintain daily contact between prisoners and the Administration. The Prisoner Liaison would be accountable to the C.P.B. and *not* to federal and provincial governments in any form.

This proposal may well be rejected out of hand by those people arguing that there are already the Citizens' Advisory Committee, the Correctional Investigator, the Inspector-General, and grievance procedures, as well as an (over)abundance of staff such as Classification, Living Unit, Parole and Probation Officers, and Health Care and Case Management Teams, and so on, to 'help' prisoners. However, we need only turn back to Chapter 2 of this book for documentation of the violence and chaos, gross incompetence and neglect that have not been eradicated, but have more likely been intensified by the mechanisms already in place.

Another innovative contribution the C.P.B. could make is a Review Panel to expedite the speedy departure of prisoners eligible for release who continue to be detained unnecessarily because of the apparent incompetence of the National Parole Board. The most uncompromising power exercised by the Criminal Justice System was best described by the late Chief Justice Bora Laskin when he characterised its National Parole Board component as "...a tyrannical authority... without precedent among administrative agencies empowered to deal with an inmate almost as if he were a puppet on a string" (Mitchell vs. the Queen, Supreme Court of Canada, 1975).

Having attended N.P.B. hearings in the capacity of an assistant to prisoners, I can attest to a Catch-22 setup that must be seen to be believed. Where the prisoners refuse to admit guilt in spite of having been convicted (and the records are beginning to reveal the authenticity of such cases), they are denied any pass programme or parole consideration regardless of the length of their sentence. The rationale is that they are refusing to show 'remorse' or accept 'treatment' for their alleged criminal tendencies.

Others who maintain an excellent prison record with no charges or violations have no assurance that their dossier will have any bearing on the N.P.B. decision, which is based on *predicting* in a non-scientific, totally unreliable procedure, whether the applicant will be a threat to the community on release. In any event, such a 'model prisoner' is often regarded as being 'manipulative', having maintained a clean record in order to secure an early parole.

For all practical purposes, the National Parole Board should resign and turn its $12.3 million budget (up eight per cent from the previous year, according to the Solicitor-General's 1982-83 Annual Report) back to the community to provide housing, jobs, and health care for released prisoners. If judges can be persuaded to return to the short, flat sentences with one-third off for good behaviour, the prisoners would know exactly when they are to be released. There would be no further need for the mind-boggling games which attend the present routine, millions of dollars in taxpayers' money would be saved, and the tensions created by one of the most hated aspects of prison life would be relieved.

With the establishment of a Review Panel, the public would have a way to participate directly in decisions affecting prisoners and the community. Further, the Community Prison Board could work to develop meaningful programmes to identify the root causes of 'crime', to assist victims, and, with the help of the Prisoner Liaison, move steadily toward the short-term goal of fewer prisons.

The role of Prisoner Liaison is not altogether a novel idea. In 1972, Professor Philip Zimbardo of Stanford University in California urged that there "...should be an Ombudsman in every prison, not under the pay or control of the prison authority but responsible only to the courts, the state legislature and the public. Such a person could report on violations of constitutional and human rights" (*Pathology of Imprisonment*, 1972).

Another area that could be investigated by a Review Panel is the Mandatory Supervision programme on which the Correctional Service of Canada spent $250 million between 1970 and 1980 "to bring Mandatory Supervision releases back to prison for mere technical violations." R.S. Ratner of the Department of Anthropology/Sociology, University of B.C., also tells us in his essay that such 'failures' "are publicly deplored [while] positive cases are rarely advertised since the successes prefer not to be observed" (*Specious Extensions of Social Control in the Canadian Penal System*, 1982).

A Review Panel might also address itself to Protective Custody Units (P.C.U.'s.) — prisons within prisons. Who are these prisoners who are kept separate from the general prisoner population, presumably for their own protection? They are those convicted of sex offences (skinners); those labelled informers (snitches); in the women's prisons, those who have abused or killed children; and, finally, those who have asked to be moved into that Unit, believing themselves to be in physical danger from other prisoners, for a variety of reasons.

We can compare the P.C.U. with two other structures in our society. First, governments must maintain a spy system, euphemistically called 'Intelligence', in foreign countries. No government, we know, can exist in the modern world without its Intelligence Department. Secondly, no police force can function effectively without its undercover agents. Police also need to recruit informers to provide information for conviction of those allegedly involved in criminal activities.

The prison also depends on its spies and informers, since the hostility between Custody and the prison population, as well as between prisoners themselves, must be constantly reinforced if the Administration is to maintain its control. Protective Custody Units set the stage and provide the actors for this tragic drama. No prison system can function without a P.C.U., or its equivalent.

An insider's version comes from an ex-prisoner in a letter dated December 1978:

> L.R. is in P.C.U. against his own will. When he was admitted he asked to be put into population but after being told he would be killed (Administration told him this) he consented to go into P.C.U. — not fully realising the implications behind being put into that environment. Since he's been there, he repeatedly asked to be put back into population, but to no avail. You might ask, why this sudden interest — especially when I tell you I didn't

know this fellow from Adam. The answer is he is not an isolated case.

There are a lot of youngsters, who upon entry, are virtually scared into P.C.U. by the Administration. They've never done time in a pen before and when confronted by these solemn-looking people and told they will be raped, killed, etc., they check in, out of fear — not realising that once in there they are branded by the population a 'dead man' — inside and outside those walls.

Now the second question you may pose is "to what advantage is this to the Administration? and why would they mark a man 'Judas' if he wasn't?" The reason the Administration puts a man's life in jeopardy is: these people (the ones who aren't dangerous sex offenders and informants of known calibre) are used to infiltrate *all* of the Medium and Minimum institutions where there are no [official] P.C.U.'s... When an informant becomes known at one institution, he is just packed off to another, if not in one province, then to another.

*And they will continue to inform, on threat of being sent back to Maximum where there is a P.C.U.*

This is the only way authorities can successfully run these institutions, and that's why they are clamouring for more candidates for P.C.U. How long do you think they could run one of these places smoothly if they had no P.C.U. element there? Why do you think the Penitentiary Service goes to such great lengths in their continuous efforts to recruit these people? Because they need them.

If they did not have them, then all the institutions in Canada would be run as tight as Maximum Security is, because they couldn't afford to run them any other way.

I think we're going to have to face reality here and state that at least a few Members of Parliament are aware of this travesty of justice, this wanton sentencing of young men to death, to murder!

Don't forget there are 25 more prisons being built and they need the troops to man the P.C.U.'s.

I think it's about time the Canadian public was made aware of the greatest 'horror' story in penitentiary history. But how do you make them aware — how can you obtain the necessary facts and figures — only a very special inquiry will obtain these results.

When supposed responsible citizens are given the power to virtually mould men into the lowest form of life, then one must ask oneself — 'how can we judge these victims of the hierarchy?'

I know you may have a hard time digesting what I am writing and I'm the first to admit that most of those in P.C.U. belong there — but there are more than a few who don't. About ten or fifteen years ago there was no such thing as P.C.U. in the Canadian Penitentiary System. Now there are over 1,000 men in them.

In January 1979, prisoners at Dorchester Penitentiary called for the total dismantling of their P.C.U. Recommendation No. 1 of their Factum reads:

(a) P.C.U. within this institution has always been a problem to the main population. Recently it has been increased in six months from forty to fifty residents. Administration does not discourage men from going there but rather they encourage the move, even for minor problems.

(b) As a result of this unit, the population has suffered many cutbacks and losses to the already small number of facilities, for example, removal of three trailers to P.C.U. and added work load to staff and liaison officers drawn to supervise the unit.

(c) The P.C.U. draws from the budget for activities, films, equipment and special needs. The population suffers the resulting shortage in most areas.

(d) The losses only encourage recruitment of this unit. It should be relocated in order to restore the morale necessary for co-existence of main population.

The Protective Custody Unit serves an important political function within the prison structure. In order to maintain their authority, penitentiary officials — many of them ex-military Intelligence — must preserve, among other controls, the P.C.U.

Established power thrives by keeping its subjects divided. For example, P.C.U.'s are breeding grounds for racism. At Oakalla, East Indian prisoners tend to be directed automatically upon admission to the P.C.U. wing. At the B.C. Pen, when East Indian guards were selected for the 'goon squad', again

167

racist tensions intensified. An already high level of racism outside is perpetuated inside.

The system exploits the complexities of sexism as well. Deprived of their outside sex partners, and confined for long, unwholesome periods of time, prisoners sometimes turn to whatever sexual release they can find. The Administration is able to use information about such intimate relationships to further coerce and thus compel participation in the 'spy' system.

Ostensibly, Administrations set up Protective Custody for the protection of certain categories of prisoners against the physical threat of others. But the real intent is to divide the prison population to a degree that prevents them from being able to cope with the hopelessness of their incarceration.

How else explain placing someone in the cell next to the brother of the man he was suspected of having 'fingered'. Appeals from the Prisoners' Rights Group (P.R.G.) to Oakalla's Director, warning of the potential revenge in this case, were ignored for months. The two prisoners were finally separated, fortunately, before a fatal stabbing.

A prisoner's life is also precarious in the general population. If the guards by-pass a cell while searching the rest of the tier, one of the occupants can be suspected of currying favour with the guards. If he is lucky he will be able to convince his cell-mates that he was being 'set up'. If he is not so fortunate, and the guards succeed in sowing suspicion against him, he faces either 'toughing it out' without being stabbed, or taking 'protection' in P.C.U.

Inevitably, there are now P.C.U.'s within P.C.U.'s — literally, a prison within a prison within a prison. These are for prisoners who must be protected against each other, even within that Unit. This is a logical proliferation of a process designed to produce people who, if they are to survive at all, will feel compelled to inform, to intimidate, to use and to fear each other — *ad infinitum*.

The essential 'divide and conquer' rule is applied in this area with considerable success. As in the world community where the device of encouraging 'colonials' to battle amongst themselves strengthens the power of the master nation, thus dividing prisoners into Maximum, Medium, and Minimum security status offers a lever to the respective Administrations which they then use with impunity. The added bonus of relegating an entire section of the prison population to the most despised status of rapists and informers further reinforces the control factor.

Proof of this strategy is the total disregard for research into the subject, as exemplified by the MacGuigan Report in 1977: "...penitentiaries, through appropriate reforms to correctional practices, can also substantially reduce or eliminate most Protective Custody requirements. The danger faced by these men, however, is not in the long run, but immediate, and a short-term solution must be sought. The suffering imposed on individuals in Protective Custody is certainly not authorised by Canadian law nor contained in the lawful sentence of any court. What happens... in Protective Custody is intolerable. Corrective action is required." Recommendation Number 57 reads:

> A small number of maximum security institutions should be used exclusively for inmates who require Protective Custody. Each such institution should have a section designed as medium security.

The result of this recommendation is that for a few brief years two prisons were set aside for Protective Custody — Saskatchewan Penitentiary in Prince Albert and Kingston Penitentiary in Ontario — with just one range for the very few P.C. women in the Prison for Women (P 4 W). The next step was to ignore the recommendation and build more prisons which were set aside for Special Handling Units *and* Protective Custody Units, albeit in separate buildings, but within the same prison compound. So there are now both an S.H.U. and a P.C. in Prince Albert, and the soon-to-be-opened Renous in New Brunswick will also combine S.H.U. and P.C. Kent in B.C. has expanded to include two more ranges of twenty-four each, one for segregation and one for Protective Custody, within the confines of a 'campus style' prison which was to be a model for future Corrections construction.

So much for 'good advice' from their own Parliamentary commissions. It is clear that something other than government inquiries and commissions are needed.

The Review Panel might also investigate another phenomenon desperately needing attention — the disproportionate number of Native Indian prisoners, who comprise approximately forty to sixty per cent of our prison population but only eight to ten per cent of the population of Canada. According to the Solicitor-General as quoted in the *Edmonton Journal*, August 29, 1984: "Statistics show Natives are much more likely to go to prison for committing the same crime than non-Natives... greater effort must be made to keep Natives who have broken the law out of prison. There are alternatives to incarceration and it is desirable to develop them." Yet when attempts have been made to alter the grim statistics, they have been quashed. A B.C. Corrections worker reported in *Monday Magazine* (March 21, 1977) that "...when I had exact figures [of the ratio of Native Indians in prison compared to the general population] compiled for inclusion in the 1974 annual Branch report, they were deleted from the final draft. The reason? 'Too controversial', I was told."

The Parliamentary Subcommittee which sat for months in 1977 listening to a stream of bitterness from Native Indian prisoners alloted one half of one recommendation to their issue:

> *Recommendation 61*: At least one separate institution should be provided for youthful offenders on a selective basis. There should be at least one wilderness camp for native peoples and other residents accustomed to life in remote areas.

A deliberate and contemptuous indifference towards Native prisoners may not have been the intention. Nevertheless, this recommendation does reflect a remarkable capacity to accept, without protest, the disaster of a race of people other than one's own.

Only after countless protests, fasts and remarkable steadfastness, have Native Indian prisoners won the right to practice their religion, and then only in a very few prisons across Canada. This right, never questioned for other denominations, permits Natives to have their Medicine Bundles, which are carried for health, protection and purity reasons, and to construct and use Sweat Lodges. However, even this tenuous victory is constantly tempered with racist insults and ill-treatment by some guards, with the full knowledge of some Wardens. For the first time in Canada, in November 1984 a Vancouver court permitted two Native Indian prisoners to have their Medicine Bundles with them in court, since they represented their 'holy bibles.'

> It's so hard, so hard sometimes to be Indian, to be in good spirits. But I pray each day. I have my 'bundle' to protect me and give me strength and a sense of purpose. (Donn W. St. Germaine, prisoner, felled by a guard's bullet on July 20, 1984)

A Prisoner Liaison would have, along with other responsibilities, the mandate to work with women prisoners. Because they account for only six per cent of all sentenced admissions to provincial custody and two per cent of all admissions to federal custody (200 women to 12,000 men) their complaints and grievances are easily overlooked. Complaints filed on behalf of some women prisoners by a reform group (and upheld by the Human Rights Commission in 1981) were reported to be:

> ...substantially redressed. [There were] alleged discriminatory practices against women regarding their access to a broader and more comprehensive range of educational, vocational and social cultural programmes, [and a] lack of institutional options across Canada... facilities and conditions of P 4 W were inferior to those available to men. (*Let's Talk*, August 15, 1984)

By enforcing accountability criteria, a Prisoner Liaison would guarantee that these rights were not only implemented, but also that they would not again be violated. The Prisoner Liaison might also question the fairness of a ruling which pays trained and experienced women prisoners who operate the Word Processing Machine a maximum $6.45 *per day*, when the equivalent job pays $15 to $20 *per hour* outside the walls; or the impression given in the same article in *Let's Talk* that indicates that there are Exchange of Services agreements with the provinces which permit women prisoners under federal jurisdiction to serve their time (two years and over) in provincial prisons closer to

171

their home communities. An examination of the facts would show that there are great inconsistencies in the application of this 'impression'.

A Community Prison Board will obviously have many thorny questions to overcome in carrying out its objectives of first guaranteeing that prisoners stay alive and well, and then expediting their speedy release wherever possible. Thorough research is necessary to discover whether there is any avenue at all within the Criminal Justice System whereby sentences passed by a court of law can be rescinded in cases where sentences are proved to be unfair and unjust, and consequently, immoral and illegal. A C.P.B. would need to discover also whether there are any means of opposing the Penitentiary Service Regulations.

The courts, legislature and the Solicitor-General's department move with amazing speed and force when it is a matter of destruction of *property*. We must find ways to act with equal speed and force when it is a matter of destruction of *human beings*.

The Government of Canada must be called to account for its refusal to abide by International Covenants which it has signed and ratified. The Amendment to the Parole Act passed in 1977 provides that when a federal prisoner's parole is revoked, the time spent outside prison on parole must be counted as time served. Although it was to be considered retroactive to that date, close to 1,000 prisoners who were denied their rights were not released. The Solicitor-General made it clear that even if the United Nations found Canada violating the Covenant, the government would not consider itself bound by the finding, because, in his own words, "we are a sovereign state."

And again, when the government was called upon to account for violations of the Canadian Charter of Rights and Freedoms, which guarantees the right to vote to every Canadian citizen, it continued to deny prisoners their rights, secure in the knowledge that there are no provisions for the United Nations to force any member state to abide by its recommendations. The Executive Director of the Alberta John Howard Society, in his brief for the granting of voting rights to prisoners, summed it up well — "...people who hold a Neanderthal mentality towards the treatment of prisoners must realise that when the prisoners are released, their actions will reflect values they've adopted in prison" (*Edmonton Journal*, May 17, 1984).

By this time it should be clear that every aspect of the prison system — whether conceived as such or not — has been a stepping stone to more heinous repression. When those in total control of the management of any institution are not held accountable, there is much scope for abuse. At this level, the 'keepers' have developed into what Amnesty International has described as

> An élite group... protecting state security against 'subversives'.... If they are aware that their acts are criminal, [they] also know that *their superiors will protect them in the unlikely event that the state attempts to support [the prisoners]*. (Emphasis added) (*Torture in the Eighties*, Amnesty International, 1984)

There should be no further delusion as to the attitudes on the part of those presently in control, who are otherwise unmoved by the wanton waste of human beings combined with the perpetuation of a fiscal folly of monumental proportions. Efforts by a Community Prison Board to remove even one layer of the system's cloak of secrecy must nevertheless continue, while guarding against being co-opted, or frustrated beyond endurance. The best antidote lies in the unfailing response from the prisoners themselves, whose sense of solidarity can be very healing:

> ...the knowledge that we are supported by friends on the outside helps to neutralise the feelings of total isolation which plague us all. Administration has been free to act in virtual secrecy, distorting the facts and denying us the right to speak as well as denying the outside community's right to listen... the aim is to set a precedent that will help safeguard the rights of prisoners in the future... there is no separating the dehumanisation in prison from corruption in legalistic systems, from the racism and violence inbred in the institutions comprising a society based on economic prosperity for business... injustice is injustice is injustice. ("Danbury: Anatomy of a Prison Strike," *Liberation*, May 1972)

May 1983 was an important landmark for those who have long been striving for a way out of the morass of the prisoner's lot. Following the inspired initiative of Dr. Ruth Morris, a former co-ordinator of the Canadian Society of Friends, the Quakers' Committee on Jails and Justice called a Conference on Prison Abolition in Toronto, Ontario. More than 400 people gathered from Canada and the U.S., and from Scotland, England, the Scandinavian countries and Australia.

The preamble to the Conference agreed that:

1) Prisons are brutalising and dehumanising institutions which have grave consequences not only for the prisoners and their families, but also for those who must administer the system and work in the prisons, and for the community itself;

2) The disadvantaged are over-represented in penal institutions;

3) These institutions are not even effective in terms of the aims of those who advocate their continued use and to protect society and deter crime;

4) The criminal law system reflects the worst values of society, and this is not only seen in the inequities of the criminal trial but also in the lack of concern for victims of crime.

One of the action proposals put forward at the Conference condemned the highly discriminatory use of prisons toward racial, cultural and ethnic minority groups in every country. Also condemned was the existence of Special Handling Units, solitary confinement, and other forms of Administrative segregation, since such behaviour is contrary to Human Rights and the United Nations Charter of Freedoms.

This Statement of Principles was accepted:

1) To inspire those already committed to prison abolition, by gathering many of us together to strengthen our mutual dedication to a world without prisons.

2) To exchange ideas and think creatively together about how to achieve prison abolition, and what conditions must go with it.

3) To educate the general public on the failure of prisons and the need for new thinking in this area.
4) To address the questions of those who believe prisons have failed but wonder about the meaning and practicality of abolishing them.

The three values underlying the Abolition Model were based on 1) economic and social justice, recognising the ties between imprisonment and the 'isms' — racism, classism, sexism and patriarchalism — that lead to oppression; 2) concern for *all* victims, recognising that many of the people who go through our Criminal Justice System are victims of oppression themselves; and 3) reconciliation.

And, to better understand how we can work towards abolition in concrete ways, the Attrition Model was adopted:

1) Moratorium on prison construction;
2) Decarceration — keeping people out of prison by pre-trial and post-trial diversion systems;
3) Excarceration — diminishing the sentence by providing alternatives to institutional confinement;
4) Restraint — for the few demonstrably dangerous cases to enable them to be treated in humane environments.

A few highlights from the published *Proceedings of the 1st International Conference on Prison Abolition:*

How to get to abolition from here... given the real world and the real people and problems in it, what can we do now that will be a practical and positive step towards a world without prisons, not just another band-aid helping the prisoning society continue to separate us into categories, and deal with social problems by labelling and punishing people. *(Ruth Morris)*

If poor people wrote the laws, might it not be possible that to cause poverty, or to keep someone in poverty, would be as much a criminal offence as it is to steal? One might speculate that if all people who evade income taxes, or who pad their expense accounts, were caught, convicted and sentenced to prison we would soon believe that crime is a middle class and upper middle class problem. *(Edgar Epp)*

The process of abolishing prisons is very complex. You cannot work only on a rational basis. You have to begin to get at people's fears and emotions, their mindsets and their world view, and when you realise that it's a prison industrial complex in the same way that it's a military industrial complex, then you realise that you're up against powerful forces. *(Rev. Virginia Mackey)*

The question also comes up whether we should abolish prisons before we start something else. Do we abolish prisons first or do we create the human system first? I suppose the attrition model... is really about creating the new before the old is abolished. And there's a great damage in that. We have to be very careful that the old system is not left intact and is not continued to be used for Blacks and Native Americans and other people who are easily identified as members of groups that we have earmarked for oppression, while we use the other system for the 'good' folks. *(Frank Durnbaugh)*

A second International Conference on Prison Abolition takes place in Amsterdam June 23-25, 1985. Sponsored by the Criminology Institute of the Free University, it "bring[s] together active participants to discuss ideas and to elaborate plans that serve as a basis for concrete actions in the near future." With equal optimism, it is expected that plans will be laid for a third International Conference in 1987, perhaps in South America.

There is a vast difference between protest and resistance. Protest is what we do when we meet together at conferences and demonstrations, to learn from one another, to assert our beliefs, and to make them known to the largest possible audience.

Resistance, on the other hand, is when we finally consider ways of putting our protests into action. Historian and critic George Woodcock explains: "...direct action is an approach that stresses the power of individuals and groups to solve their own problems without involvement of government or any other forms of authority. Such action is often taken as a last resort, after all the legitimate channels — voting, petitions, lobbying — have been tried to no avail" (*Vancouver Sun*, February 28, 1983).

In an inverse sense, it can be said that the Canadian Government also practised 'direct action' when it used the War Measures Act in 1970 to jail hundreds of Québecois(e) without laying any charges. At that time, according to the *Whig Standard* (August 18, 1984), the present Minister of External Affairs let it be known that he "...considered it sinister when Canadian citizens may be thrown in jail without charge... sinister when the House of Commons is promised that it will receive an explanation about why these actions took place, yet never receives that kind of explanation." Years have passed and this 'sinister' mystery has yet to be solved.

When Bill 9 (C.S.I.S.), which threatens our citizens' rights, was being hotly debated, we were assured that the right to dissent in a democracy was still ours, and would never be challenged. Legitimate dissent was also proclaimed to be one of the political virtues of our democratic system. Surely the time has come to consider implementing the 'moral imperative to disobey immoral laws.'

Howard Zinn's warning in 1968 is just as relevant today as it was then:

> When laws seriously encroach on human rights, they should be violated... that some conditions are so intolerable that they may require violations of otherwise reasonable laws. If the effect of civil disobedience is to break down in the public's mind the totalitarian notion that laws are absolute and always to be obeyed, then this is healthy for the growth of democracy... When unjust decisions are accepted, injustice is sanctioned and perpetuated... (*Disobedience and Democracy*, 1968)

One need look no further for such additional sanctions than the Manifesto presented by 53 Nobel Prize winners in 1981. They urged the world's poor,

> ...victims of the international political and economic disorder which prevails in the world today to practise civil

disobedience to fight the threat of mass starvation... If the helpless take their fate into their own hands, if increasing numbers refuse to obey any law other than fundamental human rights, the most basic of which is the right to life, if the weak organise themselves and use the few but powerful weapons available to them... it is certain that an end could be put to this catastrophe in our time. (*The Province*, January 25, 1981)

It is therefore time to examine the choice which must be made by prisoner and non-prisoner alike. When we call attention to the lawlessness of the prison bureaucracy but fail to challenge its very existence, we contribute to its continuance. It is time to make use of the abundance of information and resources, with skill and determination. One way to 'unfreeze' this situation is to consider acts of civil disobedience so that the commitment to 'the sanctity of life' will begin to have some meaning.

Part of the process of working towards the abolition of prisons is finding ways to inform and involve the public, to demonstrate that no longer should prisons be considered someone else's problem. Prisoners come from the same communities and suffer the same massive cutbacks in housing, schools and health care that we all do. And it is the communities that have to finally come to grips with more humane ways to eliminate the unsecurity of their lives than by calling for more and tougher prisons.

# Conclusion

*Justice no longer takes public responsibility for the violence that is bound up with its practice.*

Michel Foucault

No one would argue that there is any comparison between the starving and dying throughout the globe and those serving time in a Canadian prison. However, what is being emphasised is that corruption and violence are no less acceptable whether sanctioned by governments or by prison authorities. Or whether the dying be from starvation or from assault and suicide.

If we are indeed facing the threat of a 'nuclear winter' — and who is to know when a computer error may take effect — more reason to pick up momentum and dare to do those things for which we might not otherwise find the courage. If, on the other hand, 'cooler heads prevail' and we continue to live in a world that can only be improved by our efforts, once more the time to start is *now*.

To challenge elected representatives and prison officials (all of whom are rewarded most handsomely from the public pocket) seems a mild gesture compared with the evil perpetrated in their name, which is accompanied by deafening silence.

Should Community Prison Boards, Prisoner Liaisons or Review Panels fail to materialise, a well-planned, sustained campaign might be considered, modelled after that of the spirited women at Greenham Common in England. For three years they have camped at the gates of an American missile base, facing physical violence, gunfire and cold winters. There are also nuns sentenced to three to five years at Alderson Women's Prison in West Virginia for having entered defence plants and damaged components of the Pershing-II missile.

It has been said that "if class consciousness is knowing which side of the fence you are on, class analysis is knowing who is there with you." Prison activists are in good cc

179

Granted, the fate of those Canadian prisoners who do survive cannot be compared with the terrible devastation in the world about us. Nor can they be considered political prisoners in the same sense as can those fighting for their freedom against foreign-supported troops. The struggle to dismantle the power structure is already a vital part of the universal battle for independence and justice.

It is no longer possible — as if it ever were — to remain indifferent to the sight of another human being encaged. One must either share the degradation or be responsible for it. In one way or another one has to be accountable, whether to conscience or to peers who do care. A well-organised citizenry could begin to attack the entrenched opposition. In their domain, environmentalists and anti-militarists are showing the way with their direct actions. The same can be done at prison gates.

The intent of this book is clear — to link the prison abolition movement with other political struggles for fundamental change. A formidable task, but one which must be tackled — with creativity, with enthusiasm, and with a passion.

# August 10th
# National Prison Justice Day

## What is August 10th — National Prison Justice Day?

A day set aside each year since 1976 when prisoners and supporters gather to respect the memory of those who have died unnatural deaths in Canadian prisons.

## What alternatives are there to imprisonment?

A good start would be decarceration, i.e. phasing out the vast majority who do not require institutionalisation. Although 85% is the generally accepted estimate, the Commissioner of Penitentiaries admits that 40% do not need to be in prison. That would mean 40% of 11,500 (Federal prison population alone), which would in turn mean approximately 4,600 prisoners would have been phased out by now. Obviously this is not being done and contributes to riots and disturbances, which happen mainly when too many people are in prison for too long.

## What of the remaining portion of prisoners?

Every effort should then be made to help them by checking out their physical, nutritional, allergic, environmental, economic and social conditions, as we know that 95% are from the socially deprived poverty class.

Much so-called criminal behaviour stems from biochemical and ecological factors. Funds should be transferred to this area instead of being squandered on psychiatric centres with their emphasis on experimental behavioural modification programmes.

## Hasn't society a right to be protected from law breakers?

Yes, of course. But does throwing them into prison really protect anyone? Or does it in reality pave the way for more violence by more people who have been incarcerated under degrading conditions, and then returned to the community more unstable than when they went in?

And, anyway, we should also be dealing with those corporate law-breakers who poison our food, rivers and air, and who violate health and safety regulations, all of which cause far more extensive injury and death than does street crime. Society also has a right to be protected from conventional and nuclear arms-makers.

## Why should prisoners be respected if they have broken the law?

Because not every prisoner is actually guilty, when the truth comes out.

Because "It is the duty of the institutional head to take all reasonable steps to ensure the safe custody of inmates committed to his(her) care." (Penitentiary Act: 1962-302, Part II, Section 2.27)

Because any threat to the safety of any prisoner is a violation of human rights, and if allowed to pass unchallenged, constitutes a threat to each of us.

## Why do we have such a large prison population?

Canada shares the record for the longest sentences — often from 10 to 25 years before parole *eligibility*, which in turn can and does mean a full life span. By the year 2000, the experts are predicting, there will be approximately 1,974 prisoners serving 10-25 years in Canadian prisons.

The longer prisoners are kept isolated from their families and community, the more difficult it is for them to readjust on release, and the more likely that they will be returned to prison. This pattern does not diminish the so-called crime rate.

Canada is undergoing severe economic crises in unemployment and inflation, resulting in cutbacks in housing, health care and social services. However, prisons remain the chief growth industry, a multi-million-dollar investment which employs tens of thousands of people

182

and is seen as a boost to the economy. We are therefore encouraging an industry whose merchandise is people!!

## What concrete changes are needed to stop prison violence?

Concerned citizens to monitor every prison and jail regularly and speak privately with staff and prisoners about their problems, and to publicise their findings.

Paroles should be granted automatically to all those who have completed their minimum sentence. All those not dangerous to themselves or to others should have their sentences commuted to make them eligible for immediate paroles.

Administrators should meet regularly with Prisoners' Committees to deal with their problems.

Legislatures should revise sentencing laws downwards to short, flat sentences, with maximum of 5-8 years, as in some other countries.

The National Parole Board should be abolished and its resources transferred to meet the community's needs, particularly in the areas of preventative projects.


**ABOLISH SOLITARY CONFINEMENT**
**ABOLISH FORCED INVOLUNTARY TRANSFERS**
**ABOLISH MANDATORY SUPERVISION**
**ABOLISH "GATING"**
**ABOLISH DOUBLE-BUNKING**
**ABOLISH PRISONS**
**REVIEW 25-YEAR SENTENCES**

*CHALLENGE SPY BILL C-9 — LEGISLATION TO CREATE THE*
*CANADIAN SECURITY INTELLIGENCE SERVICE (C.S.I.S.)*
*A DANGEROUS THREAT TO ALL CIVIL AND HUMAN RIGHTS*

# Declaration of Stockholm
# 11 December 1977

The Stockholm Conference on the Abolition of the Death Penalty, composed of more than 200 delegates and participants from Africa, Asia, Europe, the Middle East, North and South America and the Caribbean region,

## Recalls That:

— The death penalty is the ultimate cruel, inhuman and degrading punishment and violates the right to life.

## Considers That:

— The death penalty is frequently used as an instrument of repression against opposition, racial, ethnic, religious and underprivileged groups.
— Execution is an act of violence, and violence tends to provoke violence.
— The imposition and infliction of the death penalty is brutalising to all who are involved in the process.
— The death penalty has never been shown to have a special deterrent effect.
— The death penalty is increasingly taking the form of unexplained disappearances, extra-judicial executions and political murders.
— Execution is irrevocable and can be inflicted on the innocent.

## Affirms That:

— It is the duty of the state to protect the life of all persons within its jurisdiction without exception.
— Executions for the purposes of political coercion, whether by government agencies or others, are equally unacceptable.
— Abolition of the death penalty is imperative for the achievement of declared international standards.

## Declares:

— Its total and unconditional opposition to the death penalty.
— Its condemnation of all executions, in whatever form, committed or condoned by governments.
— Its commitment to work for the universal abolition of the death penalty.

## Calls Upon:

— Non-governmental organisations, both national and international, to work collectively and individually to provide public information materials directed towards the abolition of the death penalty.
— All governments to bring about the immediate and total abolition of the death penalty.
— The United Nations unambiguously to declare that the death penalty is contrary to international law.*

---

* Amnesty International, Conference on the Abolition of the Death Penalty.

# Bibliography

American Friends Service Committee, *Struggle for Justice: A Report on Crime and Punishment in America*. New York: Hill & Wang, 1971.

Amnesty International, *Torture in the Eighties*. London: Amnesty International Publications, 1984.

Archambault Theatre Group, *No Big Deal!* Translated by David Homel. Toronto: Exile Editions, 1982.

Cormier, Bruno M., *The Watcher and the Watched*. Montréal: Tundra Books, 1975.

Culhane, Claire, *Barred from Prison: A Personal Account*. Vancouver: Pulp Press, 1979.

"Danbury: Anatomy of a Prison Strike," *Liberation* Magazine, May 1972 (New York).

Davis, Angela Y., *If They Come in the Morning*. New York: Signet/NAL, 1971.

Fitzgerald, Mike, and Joe Sim, *British Prisons*. Oxford: Basil Blackwell Publishers, 1979.

Gheerbrant, Alain, *The Rebel Church in South America*. Harmondsworth: Penguin, 1974.

Gosselin, Luc, *Prisons in Canada*. Montréal: Black Rose Books, 1982.

Hewitt, Marsha, and Dimitrios Roussopoulos, eds., *1984 And After*. Montréal: Black Rose Books, 1984.

Jackson, Michael, *Prisoners of Isolation: Solitary Confinement in Canada*. Toronto: University of Toronto Press, 1983.

*Jericho: Newsletter of the National Moratorium on Prison Construction*, Winter 1982 (Unitarian Universalist Service Committee, Washington, D.C.).

Kelk, C., "The Humanity of the Dutch Prison System and the Prisoners' Consciousness of Their Legal Aid," *Contemporary Crisis 7*, 1983 (Amsterdam).

Kidron, Michael, and Ronald Segal, *New State of the World Atlas, 1984*. London: Heinemann Education Books, 1984.

Lappé, Collins & Kinley, *Aid as Obstacle*. San Francisco: Institution for Food and Development Policy, 1980.

*Let's Talk*, staff tabloid of Correctional Service of Canada (C.S.C.), Ottawa.

Margolis, Emmanuel, in *Connecticut Bar Journal*, Vol. 46, 1972 (Rocky Hill, Conn.).

McBride, Kenneth, "The Chemistry of Violence," *Queen's Quarterly*, Spring 1984 (Kingston, Ont.).

Mitford, Jessica, *Kind and Usual Punishment: The Prison Business*. Toronto: Random House of Canada, 1979.

Prison Research Education Action Project (P.R.E.A.P.) *Instead of Prisons: A Handbook for Abolitionists*. Syracuse, N.Y.: P.R.E.A.P., 1976.

Reasons, Ross & Paterson, *Assault on the Worker: Occupational Health & Safety in Canada*. Toronto: Butterworths, 1981.

*The Facts*, Special Peace Issue, May 1984 (Canadian Union of Public Employees (C.U.P.E.), Burnaby, B.C.).

Zimbardo, Philip, *Pathology of Imprisonment*. New York: Society, 1972.

Zinn, Howard, *Disobedience and Democracy*. New York: Vintage Books, 1968.

# Special Sources

*(Reports, Documents, etc.)*

Dec. 24, 1975     Report of the Study Group on Dissociation (J. A. Vantour)

Feb. 21, 1976     The Just and Legitimate Demands of the Archambault Guys (The Archambault Manifesto)

June 15, 1976     Report of Inquiry, Millhaven Incident, 3 Nov. 1975 (Inger Hansen)

1977     Report to Parliament by the Sub-Committee on the Penitentiary System in Canada (Mark MacGuigan)

Oct. 24, 1979     Speech Notes, D.R. Yeomans, Commissioner of Corrections, C.S.C., to The Institute on Donations and Public Affairs Research, Toronto

Aug. 4, 1982     Report of the Inspector-General's Special Inquiry into Riot, Archambault Institution (A. F. Wrenshall)

Sept. 23, 1982     Report to the International Human Rights Law Group, Washington, D.C. (Charles E. M. Kolb)

Nov. 3, 1982     Report from the Moderator of the United Church of Canada on Visits to Archambault Prison (Sept. 9 & 30, 1982) by the Right Reverend Clarke MacDonald

Nov. 5, 1982     Letter from the Reverend Wayne A. Smith, Moderator of the 108th General Assembly, The Presbyterian Church of Canada

Dec. 16, 1982     Report to International Federation of Human Rights, Paris, France (Thierry Maleville)

Jan. 16, 1983     Report of Interviews, Jan. 5, 1983, with Five Prisoners who Allege Abuses Following the

189

# Index

192

# LAW AND
# ANARCHISM

## edited by
## Thom Holterman and
## Henc van Maarseveen

*"1984 is a good year to read these perceptive essays on law
and justice in anarchist thought. Lawyers should read it too... an
anarchist understanding of law and its structures must increase the
chance that justice will be done, in and out of court."*

**Clayton Ruby, lawyer**

Law and anarchism are usually seen as being diametrical
opposites, but in this intriguing collection of essays the
editors make the case that anarchism cannot ignore and avoid
law and that jurisprudence cannot be disregarded.

The contributors deal with law in a wide sociological
sense as the totality of rules of all sorts which exist in a
society. Charging that the absolute rejection of law has laid
anarchists open to the most absurd charges, the editors have
gathered a wealth of reflections on the sources of social
authority arising from a revolution based on anarchist
principles.

What is the relation between the organized sanction of a
self-governing organization and the notion of law? What is
the relationship between direct action and the law and how
can direct action change the law in such a way as to promote
anarchist ideas and the anarchist society?

*Contents include:* Introduction by Clayton Ruby; Thoughts
on an Anarchist Theory of Law and the State; Anarchism
and the Theory of Political Law; Anarchism and Legal Rules;
Direct Action, Law and Anarchism; Natural Right in the
Political Philosophy of P.J. Proudhon; and Kropotkin on
Law.

Professors Holterman and van Maarseveen teach at the
Faculty of Social Science, Erasmus University, Rotterdam.

216 pages
**Paperback ISBN: 0-919619-08-9**      **$12.95**
**Hardcover ISBN: 0-919619-10-X**      **$22.95**
Law/Philosophy/Politics

# FRIENDLY FASCISM

## The New Face of Power in America

### by Bertram Gross

*"At a time of escalating political uncertainty, when the forces of totalitarianism threaten once more to crawl out of the American woodwork,* **Friendly Fascism** *is a powerful tool — better yet, a weapon — that can help us avert a distinctly unfriendly future."*

**Alvin Toffler**

*"This is the best thing I've seen on how America might go fascist democratically.* **Friendly Fascism** *offers a very clear exposition of where America is, and how we got there."*

**William Shirer**

Widely acclaimed and hotly debated, this provocative and original look at current trends in the United States presents a grim forecast of a possible totalitarian future. The author shows how the chronic problems faced by the U.S. in the late twentieth century require increasing collusion between Big Business and Big Government in order to "manage" society in the interests of the rich and powerful. This "friendly fascism", Gross argues, will probably lack the dictatorships, public spectacles, and overt brutality of the classic varieties of Germany, Italy, and Japan, but has at its root the same denial of individual freedoms and democratic rights. No one who cares about the future of democracy, in the U.S. and around the world, can afford to ignore the frightening possibilities for *Friendly Fascism.*

In a final section, he shows how, by developing our society's potential for democracy rather than despotism, we can counteract these trends.

410 pages
**Paperback ISBN: 0-920057-23-3**                    **$14.95**
**Hardcover ISBN: 0-920057-22-5**                    **$24.95**
Politics/Sociology
Publication date: October 1984

# RADICAL PRIORITIES

## by Noam Chomsky

### edited by C.P. Otero

### 2nd Revised Edition

*"...For those who desire a fuller picture of Chomsky's fascinating political scholarship, his* **Radical Priorities** *is to be recommended... [it] contains a fine essay on Chomsky by Carlos Otero."*

**Harvard International Review**

*"...One welcomes [this book], which promises to illustrate Chomsky's 'political and social philosophy'... Of course, Chomsky's writing is always rewarding — any five pages... are worth the price of the Volume.* **Radical Priorities** *is another valuable collection of Chomsky's political and social criticism."*

**The Village Voice**

The world-famous linguist at his best. This collection of Noam Chomsky's political writings — the first since 1973 and ignored by the mainstream reviewing media — brings together some of his most important reflections. Many pieces appear for the first time together in English. A broad range of subjects is covered with a view to alerting people about the problems humanity is facing and possible solutions we can undertake.

In the introduction, C.P. Otero lucidly presents an analysis and overview of Chomsky's social and political philosophy unavailable elsewhere. For the first time, the roots of Chomsky's politics are examined in relation to this theory of linguistics.

This book is invaluable for any general reader who would like to make sense out of the daily press. The second revised edition contains new important essays.

Prof. C.P. Otero teaches linguistics at the University of California, Los Angeles.

306 pages
**Paperback ISBN: 0-920057-17-9**      $14.95
**Hardcover ISBN: 0-920057-16-0**      $25.95
Politics/Philosophy/Sociology

# 1984 AND AFTER...

### edited by
## Marsha Hewitt and
## Dimitrios I. Roussopoulos

With the ominous year of 1984 in mind as a social reality more than a calendar year, this collection of essays brings together some of the most distinguished contemporary critics of authoritarian tendencies in our society. The historical, political and intellectual problems that gave rise to Orwell's great book are examined with viewpoints spanning the gamut of serious opinion. The authors offer a fresh and provocative analysis of authoritarianism and its libertarian alternatives.

Contributors include George Woodcock, Murray Bookchin, Noam Chomsky, Frank Harrison, Stephen Schecter, Jean Ellezam, Jean-Pierre Deslauriers, Yolande Cohen, Claire Culhane, John Clark, and Robert Mayo.

200 pages
**Paperback ISBN: 0-920057-29-2**  $12.95
**Hardcover ISBN: 0-920057-28-4**  $22.95
Current Affairs/Politics

Printed in Canada